PASSAGE
TO
FREEDOM

First published by O Books, 2008
O Books is an imprint of John Hunt Publishing
Ltd., The Bothy, Deershot Lodge, Park Lane,
Ropley, Hants, SO24 0BE, UK
office1@o-books.net
www.o-books.net

Distribution in:

UK and Europe
Orca Book Services
orders@orcabookservices.co.uk
Tel: 01202 665432 Fax: 01202 666219 Int. code
(44)

USA and Canada
NBN
custserv@nbnbooks.com
Tel: 1 800 462 6420 Fax: 1 800 338 4550

Australia and New Zealand
Brumby Books
sales@brumbybooks.com.au
Tel: 61 3 9761 5535 Fax: 61 3 9761 7095

Far East (offices in Singapore, Thailand, Hong
Kong, Taiwan)
Pansing Distribution Pte Ltd
kemal@pansing.com
Tel: 65 6319 9939 Fax: 65 6462 5761

South Africa
Alternative Books
altbook@peterhyde.co.za
Tel: 021 555 4027 Fax: 021 447 1430

Text copyright Dawn Mellowship 2008

ISBN: 978 1 84694 078 1

Printed in the US by Maple Vail

O Books operates a distinctive and ethical publishing philosophy in all areas of its business, from its global network of authors to production and worldwide distribution.
No trees were cut down to print this particular book. The paper is 100% recycled, with 50% of that being post-consumer. It's processed chlorine-free, and has no fibre from ancient or endangered forests.
This production method on this print run saved approximately thirteen trees, 4,000 gallons of water, 600 pounds of solid waste, 990 pounds of greenhouse gases and 8 million BTU of energy. On its publication a tree was planted in a new forest that O Books is sponsoring at The Village www.thefourgates.com

PASSAGE
TO
FREEDOM

DAWN MELLOWSHIP

BOOKS

Winchester, UK
Washington, USA

Jesus said, "If your leaders say to you, 'Behold, the kingdom is in the sky,' then the birds in the sky will get there before you. If they say to you, 'It is in the sea,' then the fish will get there before you.

"Rather, the kingdom is inside you and outside you. When you know yourselves then you will be known, and will understand that you are children of the living Father. But if you do not know yourselves, then you live in poverty, and embody poverty."

The Gospel of Thomas, Saying 3, CODEX II: 32-33

Contents

PREFACE   XV

INTRODUCTION   XVII

PART ONE   SPIRITUAL BONDING   1

   1. Creating Connections   6
   2. Finding Direction, Being Guided   14

PART TWO   FACING LIFE, BEING TRUTH   23

   3. Understanding Anger   28
   4. Lifting Worry   39
   5. Being Thankful   52
   6. Taking Responsibility   58
   7. Knowing The Truth   67

PART THREE   SELF HEALING, SELF LOVE   75

   8. Releasing The Past   81
   9. Self-Acceptance   88
   10. Expressing Your True Self   95
   11. Healthy Living   102

PART FOUR   BEING TRUTH, LIVING TRUTH   113

   12. Being Balanced   119
   13. Being Aware   125
   14. Being Love   133
   15. Accepting Your Higher Path   143
   16. Being Truth   149

PART FIVE   BEING WISE, HAVING FAITH   155

   17. Being Wise   161
   18. Having Faith   172

PART SIX   BEING THE WAY   183

   19. A Guide To Others   185

PART SEVEN   ENLIGHTENMENT   203

   20. At One   205

PART EIGHT   THE REIKI WAY   221

   21. Reiki Lights The Way   223

CONCLUSION   **233**

List of Techniques

	page
Forming Connections	9
Uniting The Trinity	12
Path Seeking	17
Guiding Light	19
Understanding Anger	33
Worry Shifter	44
Problem Solving	49
Grateful Living	56
Seeing Consequences	62
Taking Responsibility	65
Facing Reality	71
Recognising and Releasing Past Guilt	86
Accepting Yourself	93
Self-Expression	100
Healthy Living	110
Balancing Act	123
Expanding Awareness	130
Allowing Unconditional Love	141
Accepting Higher Path Gracefully	147
Your True Self	154
Shaping Wisdom	166
Being Wisdom	169
Fostering Faith	177
Keeping Faith	180
Strength and Guidance in Helping Others	194
Standing Back	197
Retaining Humility	199
Being The way	201
Enlightenment Transition	212
Universal knowledge	214
Basking in Light	218

Acknowledgements

I sincerely believe that nothing in life happens by accident and everyone who has crossed my path, has influenced my path in one way or another. To my perfect Andrew Chrysostomou, who showed me my higher path and consistently helps me to believe in myself, who loves me unconditionally and a great deal more, I am eternally grateful. I love you forever. To Mikao Usui who is no longer with us, thank you so much for discovering the beautiful art of Reiki, your spiritual gift was truly phenomenal and I hope I am doing enough justice to your spiritual work. To my brother Peter Brotherston, you are an amazing, funny and caring person, you have helped me in so many ways and I will never forget that, thank you. To Caroline Kail, you filled me with hope where I felt none and reminded me of where I should be heading. Your help was invaluable, thank you. To my mother, thank you for bringing me into this world. To everyone else who has helped me on my journey, I am truly grateful.

Dedication

This book is dedicated to God and Andrew Chrysostomou for their never ending support, guidance, love, strength and beauty and to Mikao Usui the founder of Reiki, who was blessed with a gift to change the lives of many. If it were not for these three, I would not be where I am today.

Preface

The world of the twenty-first century is such a thirsty world. Sometimes, this thirst is beautiful because millions of people are embarking upon a spiritual quest, searching for the true meaning of life, searching for their souls. At other times, the thirst is agonising because people are needlessly suffering at the mercy of other humans, or at the mercy of their own corporeal misery. We all have the power within us, to be set free.

Frequently we misunderstand freedom, but when freedom is truly found, it is exquisitely beautiful, too beautiful to express in the poverty of language. The passage to freedom can be discovered by attaining 'oneness' or 'completeness,' by connecting with our higher selves, the long suffering souls that throughout our lives endure our very often detrimental physical existence.

To connect to these souls can involve embarking upon a long arduous journey, or merely taking one simple step forward. That really depends on us. The easy answer is 'seek and you will find.' Whoever bravely sets foot on the journey to enlightenment, if they are earnest in their searching, will rightly be shown the way. However, so many people miss the signs they are given, or are so distant from their higher selves that their reaching out is fruitless, because they are utterly blind to the truth. Most people are unaware that they are walking around in a dream, utterly drunk on their physical existence. It is only when we are connected with our higher selves, our true Divine nature and the Universe that our eyes are opened wide and we awake from our slumber.

"With this book I cordially invite you to take a journey with me. I invite you to be free. Whoever wishes to take this path read this book and follow me."

Dawn Mellowship

Introduction

We are all on a path, whether we know it, understand it or believe in it. The potential is there for us to nourish our souls, to gain wisdom and to achieve 'oneness.' This is a choice we all have to make for ourselves, as individuals. Do we want to grow spiritually, or are we content with a purely physical existence?

We all have the potential to change our lives. If we remember nothing else in life, we should remember this. Some people may claim to be happy neglecting their spiritual nature and gear their lives towards pursuing their physical wants: earning more money, fulfilling their desires, amassing bigger and better products. Yet, if they were to question whether this is really their chosen path, they may find the answer wildly diverging from their initial expectations. The path we choose begets the prevailing negative or positive consequences. We all have to live by the decisions we make in life and if anyone needs to stop for a second to question their choices, then they have made the wrong ones. If anyone has to even contemplate whether they are truly happy or not, then they have not achieved fulfilment.

Our physical bodies are transitory vessels, escorting us on a journey that can appear long, troublesome and riddled with grief. However, this life we have here on earth, the whole existence of the world, is but the blink of an eye compared to our entire journey. In that brief moment when the eye closes, we have made thousands of choices and as the eye rapidly opens again, we must accept the aftermath. We would all be wise to seek our higher paths and free ourselves from the oppressive chains we have created.

For those exploring their true spiritual nature, the task can be daunting. The easiest answer is 'seek and you will find,' but in the twenty-first century the lust for power and yearning for spirituality are locked in a battle of wills. Sometimes, they become fused because humanity is prone to seizing authority. Are the spiritual truly spiritual or are they trying to deceive us? We are torn between those who justly try to help us and those who prey on our vulnerabilities, because they know that we are searching, and they so desperately long to lead us in the wrong direction.

The simplest way out of this formidable quandary, is to understand that our intuition is our greatest guide, our life long devoted companion who calls out to us to hear the truth. We can all access that intuition; we can listen to our inner guidance, learn from the teachings of our higher self, follow our higher path and discover just what we have been missing for so long.

So, to all who reach out for their soul but cannot find what they are looking for, I offer a guide to show you a path that I chose to take, that you too can take, a path to freedom.

Wisdom comes from knowing when you are truly free. Many people are under the misconception that they are living 'wild and free,' when in reality they are in servitude to their own human nature. Most of the images we project are a far cry from our true spiritual selves. We are too busy trying to please others, clinging onto a lifetime of accumulated guilt or simply ignoring our true purpose. This is easy enough for any of us to acknowledge, but much harder to let go of. We have a lifetime of conditioning to break away from, but rest assured that it can be done.

So, bearing all this in mind, I pondered for a while because my journey was tough and it took a very brave man and my faith in God to help me attain my true potential. I was constrained by the traits of my parents and peers and as I undertook my spiritual path, confusion reigned. I had spent my life pursuing the wrong goals, damaging my health and my higher self. Fortunately, undertaking a Reiki course re-connected me to my true spiritual nature and through learning tough lessons and understanding my past, I was able to walk out of the cage I had crafted for myself. Reiki is one means of discovering our true inner potential and walking on the path towards enlightenment. Yet still, not everyone will learn Reiki and of those who do choose to walk this path, not everyone will use it. I needed to create a Universal guide, a method for revealing the Divine reality inside each person, the reality that if everyone was honest, they long to achieve.

It was after this that I knew. I was writing an article and the words readily flowed without me having to muster one thought, the article turned into a book, a guidebook to enable anyone who is searching for their soul in earnest, who has determination, dedication, the will to be all that they can be.

The book is divided into chapters describing how to achieve the various goals required to embark on the road to enlightenment and true freedom. Each chapter discusses the importance of the particular goal in question, gives exercises to help you achieve that goal and if necessary, explains why those exercises need to be performed.

I felt that I could not write this book about freedom and enlightenment without featuring a chapter on Reiki, the astonishing Japanese healing art that performs what would seem to most to be miracles. Reiki changed my life radically, from the second I set foot on my journey to the Reiki teacher's house. From that moment onwards, my life underwent such drastic, mesmerising transformations that seated me firmly on my spiritual path and gave me insights that I could only ever have dreamed of in the past. Learning Reiki is akin to being struck with Divine revelation, in fact it is this very thing. Reiki has the power to take a life of darkness and turn on the Light, so that the true knowledge of oneself and the Universe can be seen.

People are often immersed in an elaborate dream and Reiki is, most truthfully, a very welcome wake up call. With diligence and continued daily practise of this healing method true enlightenment can be attained. Reiki can help absolutely any condition and brings into perfect unison the physical, emotional and spiritual bodies, in order for us to realise the sublime 'oneness' we all secretly wish for. Reiki is a clinical therapy, spiritual path, a ubiquitous energy and possesses the unique ability to fast track anyone who chooses to learn this healing art to a strong re-connection with his or her higher nature. Thereafter, with dedicated self-healing, enlightenment can eventually be attained. As the founder of Reiki Mikao Usui stated,

"Reiki....the Secret Method of Inviting Happiness, the Miraculous Medicine of All Diseases."

For your reference, when I refer to the Light of the Universe, the Light, or the Universe in this book I am referring to God. Do not be afraid of this word. I use it only because language is inept to describe the reality of this concept. Words are unimportant in that sense. In my eyes, God and religion are not synonymous. I view God as an intelligent and creative energy. This energy is all around us and within us, only some of us have locked this energy in a dark box and forgotten its existence. Using the Light in the exercises is intended to aid you in accessing the key to this lock and allowing the Light within you to shine forth radiantly for all to see. Do not worry if you have no belief in any creative energy, the exercises provided will still assist you in accessing your inner wisdom.

The breathing exercises used, are to help you exude calmness and tranquillity and more importantly, to train you to breathe correctly. Many people only use a fraction of their full lung capacity. On every inhalation you make, oxygen is pouring into your body, you are breathing in the very essence of life. On every exhalation you make, carbon dioxide and toxins are being expelled from your body. If you do not breathe correctly, these toxins will accumulate and this can prove to be incredibly detrimental to your health and well-being. Breathe deeply and slowly. Learn to nourish your body.

The hand positions are a feature of Reiki and allow the Light and certain affirmations to be concentrated in specific areas of your body for healing purposes.

Seiza is a standard sitting position, used on formal occasions in Japan, where you rest your bottom on your feet, keeping your back straight. This position is also used in many forms of Japanese martial arts and in traditional Reiki for various meditation techniques.

Agura is an informal method of sitting cross-legged, used in the Japanese culture.

Gassho is a hand position that is very much a part of Reiki (it is the Japanese word for joining your hands together in prayer). This very action creates a bond within you, when used with the appropriate exercises.

Visualisation and intention are highly important. They are used in Reiki and form a vital part of the exercises in this book. Dr Glen Rein PhD. (Quantam Biology Research Labs) has carried out research into healing tumour cells, using intention and visualisation. He discovered that by utilising the appropriate intention and visualisation on cancer cells in petri dishes, their growth was inhibited by an astonishing 39%. Where a visualisation was used of the cancer cells growing, they increased in number by 15%.[1]

When you use the visualisations and intentions (or affirmations) in this book, do so with meaning and purpose. Place all the effort you can muster into these techniques. Initially, it may be difficult, but as you get used to meditating every day, your confidence and abilities will dramatically improve.

The various affirmations used in this book should be recited a particular number of times. This is not without purpose, for numbers have a great significance, thus I felt it essential to explain to you why I have used the designated numbers in each exercise.

The number one represents the beginning of life, the Creator, the part of God that resides within us.

The number three alludes to both creative power and spiritual growth, signifying the tripartite nature of the body, mind and soul. It is the beginning, the middle and the end: birth, life, death and the essence of the soul.

The number five is symbolic of the meeting point inside of humans that links the heaven and the earth. It suggests heightening of the five senses.

The number seven, used extensively in the meditation exercises, is the number of the Universe or macrocosm and is

---

[1] Rein, Dr Glen, Ph.D (Quantum Biology Research Labs), 1992, *Effects Of Intentionality On DNA Synthesis In Cultured Tumour Cells.*

associated with enlightenment, 'oneness,' 'completeness,' and the flawless unison of the physical, emotional and spiritual bodies. It is perfection and the embodiment of transcendence.

The number nine signifies perfection and the Kingdom of God. It is a very sacred number.

The number seventeen represents God, or if you prefer the Universe, the One that created the three, that created the four, etc combined with totality. That which created all things, will subsume those things back within the One.

The number twenty-one represents the conquering of our human nature, replaced then with intuitive awareness, a connection to the higher spiritual self.

To complete each of the exercises, I recommend that you always bow to God or the Universe as a sign of respect and gratitude for all the lessons you have received in life and for the gift of developing wisdom.

Above all, be very gentle and patient with yourself. Allow yourself to truly understand. Frustration, impatience and hastiness will only serve to stall your progress.

I sincerely hope that you enjoy reading this book and that it allows you to find your intuition and to grasp your inner wisdom. I implore you; do not believe what I have said purely because it is written in this book. Do not believe what anyone else says purely because they have written it in a book. But, if you peruse the words and they concur with your intuition, then take what you need from them, until you are guided further.

"The Light of the Universe is within you, do not hide from the Light, but rather hold the Light in your hands like a precious jewel and carry it with you all the time that you may always seek and speak the truth of that Light and be drenched in it's beauty."

Dawn Mellowship

Spiritual Bonding

"And you will know the truth, and the truth will make you free."

John 8:32

Introduction to Part One

"Without a spiritual connection, with no Light to guide our way, we are utterly lost. When you seek, if you see the Light, embrace it, let it be your guide and never let it go."

Changing your life for the better is always very challenging. Sometimes, this challenge can appear monolithic and it seems easier to retreat into your shell and quietly shy away from the responsibility of taking that step towards transformation. The important thing to remember is that those small steps count and if you are brave enough to take just one, before you know it you will have taken hundreds. You will look back to that first step and marvel at how much you have grown spiritually and emotionally, as a human being and as a soul.

Remember, this life here is a journey and long and hard as it may sometimes seem it is a truly beautiful one, a journey worth taking. Try not to think in terms of beginnings and endings because life is a circle, your soul is eternal. Even when you feel you have reached the pinnacle of your soul's potential, another mountain will arise before you and a new journey will commence. Savour every single moment of your spiritual awakening and know that as long as you remain on your spiritual path, enlightenment and true happiness will one day be yours. Be proud of your spiritual achievements and make good choices.

This first chapter of the book is all about taking that very first step. So, take a long deep breath and if you are serious about your self-development and raising your spiritual awareness, then read on and practise each meditation and exercise diligently and with consciousness. It isn't just about going through the motions, be aware of every single moment and every single aspect of the exercises and of your life. You are not just chanting affirmations or waving your arms around aimlessly, each movement has a distinct purpose, each word carries energy and every visualisation is creating a positive mindset. Be aware of your thoughts and actions, there are always consequences.

This chapter will help you to forge a spiritual bond with yourself. Our life experiences and negative patterns of behaviour can often disconnect us from our true higher selves and intuition. The key to progressing on your spiritual path is tapping back into your true spiritual nature, awakening the voice of your intuition. Stay patient and endeavour not to rush through the chapters. This is all about you taking time for yourself and raising your awareness, in a time frame that is suitable for you. Only move onto the next chapter when you feel entirely ready.

Once your intuition has grown and you can hear that inner voice talking to you and trying to steer you in the right direction, you need to be able to accurately construe and follow your spiritual guidance. The second part of Chapter One will help you to understand the guidance of the Universe and your intuition. It is essential not just to listen to your intuition, but also, to take heed of its valuable messages. Your intuition is never wrong. It will guide you where others would fail you. Always trust your intuition above anything else.

Finding direction in your life, your direction, will give you your sense of purpose. When you finally learn exactly why you were put on this earth, it becomes much easier to take those steps and follow your higher path in life.

Enjoy this chapter. It is time to start trusting in what **you** know. You know a lot more than you realise!

Chapter One

Creating Connections

When we are born into this world, we lay blissfully nurtured in our mothers' wombs, possessing completeness, perfection. We are at one with ourselves and at one with creation. The departure into a cold and harsh world, is, our first rude awakening. The physical, emotional and spiritual bodies that held fast together in paradise begin a process of being tested and of receiving constant lessons.

If we have determinedly held on tight to these earliest bonds throughout our lives, then we have served ourselves well, we have never lost our connection with our true spiritual nature. If living life has taken its toll, if our relationships and environmental interactions have detrimentally impacted on our once united trinity of wholeness, then we have become disconnected. Henceforth, our lives become a constant battle. Our physical selves cannot reconcile their demands with our emotional selves. Our spiritual selves can communicate with neither. Our intuition shouts, in fact it screams, but we have become so disconnected that we cannot hear its desperate pleas. If we do hear, it is but a brief and transient moment and we defy our intuition with our crushing reasoning. The voices in the recesses of our heads whisper as much as they can, "we have gone in the wrong direction, we are lost!" We in turn shake our heads, the egos creep in and bellow, "We are not lost, we know precisely where we are going."

This beautiful bond can be broken for a whole lifetime and the individual will spend many more lifetimes trying to retrieve the missing link. Time and again, they will trawl through life pursuing the same misguided path, missing the same Universal signs and then in indignant resignation, they will sigh one day and say, "where did it all go wrong?"

We each have within us a glorious glowing Light, a buttress for us throughout our lives despite our shortcomings. Yet, we turn down the dimmer switch until the Light is barely a flicker. If we are not terribly careful, that Light will burn out completely. This is a word to the wise, set the Light free. We cannot hope to foster the splendour of human compassion if we are disconnected human beings, with lost limbo bound souls. A disconnected person cannot fathom intuition from thought or rationality from emotion, or desire from love, or want from need. Thus, they will want everything they have never needed and want nothing they truly need. It is the burden of much of humanity from which we must all seek emancipation.

Thus it follows, our most important lesson in life is to re-unite the bond we have broken, to bring our disconnected physical, emotional and spiritual bodies back into unison. This unison is what is known as enlightenment. While these three bodies float apart and pull us in conflicting directions, we have no hope of achieving true fulfilment or freedom. When we achieve enlightenment our intuition, our logic and our physical bodies are heading in the same direction. Thinking and intuition become one and the same, instead of disparate adversaries. We become one perfect circle, instead of broken jigsaw puzzles. We can separate fact from fiction, our wants from our needs and then embark on a wondrous passage to freedom for all eternity.

Below I have cited two exercises to help you re-connect to your higher self. The first exercise, called Forming Connections, will allow you to become absorbed in the stars above, floating tranquilly through outer space, allowing you to rise above your daily existence.

You will become absorbed in bright white healing Light, which will help you to see more clearly and quieten your chattering mind, so that using affirmation, visualisation and intention you can re-gain or strengthen your connection. If you practise this technique daily for long enough you should feel that your path in life becomes more guided, your intuition will flourish and it will be easier to make good decisions for your personal development and growth.

The second exercise, entitled Uniting the Trinity, is much more powerful than the first and these should thus be used in sequence. This technique will allow the connection of body, mind and soul to be deeply ingrained and ensure that this unity is maintained throughout your daily life. By touching your navel and forehead and lodging affirmations in these areas, you are forming an incredibly cohesive bond between your physical and spiritual self, to allow the two to communicate more freely.

Creating a connection is the very first stage towards fulfilling your true potential. Without a connection we are utterly lost. We make bad choices in life and get dragged off in the wrong direction, because we cannot hear that inner voice. To hear it we must be joined with our soul. You will not need to ask when you are connected because when you are, you will know it, from within. Make a real commitment to yourself to free that inner Divine spark and see where it takes you.

Exercises

Forming Connections

1. Sit down comfortably either on the floor in seiza (on your knees with your bottom resting on your heels) (Fig 1.1) or in agura (cross-legged) (Fig 1.2) or on a chair (Fig 1.3). Make sure your back is straight. Have your hands palms facing upwards, in your lap.

2. Gently close your eyes and visualise yourself happily floating in outer space with nothing else around you but the galaxies, stars and the endless dark skies. Breathe slowly and deeply, breathing in through your nose, into your stomach and out of your mouth.

3. Visualise a bright white Light, so bright it is almost impossible to look at, coming down through space as far up as the eye can see. Visualise the Light entering the crown of your head from above, like a radiant beam. Allow the Light to enter your entire body from your head, through to the tips of your toes. As you breathe out, feel the Light pulsating through your body. Do this for a few minutes until you feel completely relaxed and lost in space!

4. As you are filled with Light, place your hands in gassho (prayer position) (Fig 1.4) in front of your chest. Silently say to yourself, or out loud, seven times, with meaning and purpose, "I open myself up to the divine will of the Universe."

5. Move your hands, still in gassho, up over the top of your head and rest them on your crown (Fig 1.5). Silently say

to yourself, or out loud, seven times, with meaning and purpose, "I open myself up to my true higher self."

6. Place your hands over your stomach, with your palms facing towards your stomach and your middle fingers meeting each other at the navel (Fig 1.6). Silently say to yourself, or out loud, seven times, with meaning and purpose, "I allow my mind, body and soul to heal; I am connected to the heaven and the earth."

7. Repeat steps 4 to 6 between three and nine times, constantly remaining focused on the Light.

8. When you have finished, breathe the white Light out of your body and back into the Universe. Place your hands in gassho by your chest again and bow to the Universe.

Fig 1.1

Fig 1.2

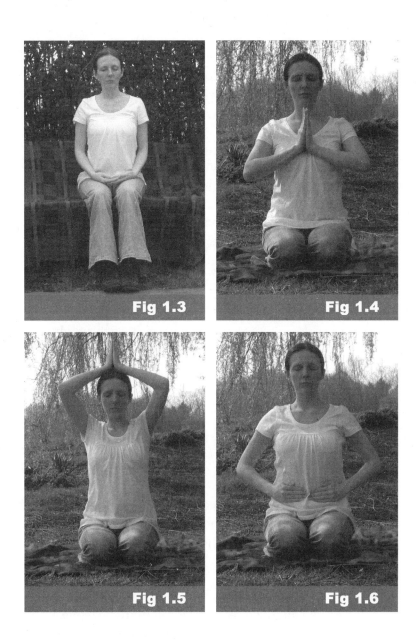

Fig 1.3

Fig 1.4

Fig 1.5

Fig 1.6

Uniting The Trinity

1. Sit down comfortably either on the floor in seiza (on your knees with your bottom resting on your heels) or in agura (cross-legged) or on a chair. Make sure your back is straight. Place your hands in gassho (prayer position) in front of your chest.

2. Take a long, deep breath in through your nose, allowing air to completely fill your lungs and reach down into your abdomen, so your abdomen swells outwards. Hold your breath for a few seconds and as you do this, visualise a powerful and bright bolt of white Light descending from the sky and shooting through your body to the ground.

3. As you breathe out, very slowly and deeply from your mouth, drawing in your stomach, visualise this Light swell up inside you until your whole body is immersed in its glow.

4. Repeat steps 2 and 3 for between five and fifteen minutes.

5. Press your hands still in gassho against the centre of your chest so your thumbs are touching your sternum.

6. Silently say to yourself, or out loud, seven times, with meaning and purpose, "The connection I forge no man can break, a holy trinity within me, an inner wisdom to awake."

7. With your hands still in gassho, press your thumbs against the middle of your forehead (third eye) (Fig 1.7) and repeat the affirmation from step 6.

8. With your hands still in gassho, press your thumbs against your navel (Fig 1.8) and repeat the affirmation from step 6.

9. Place your hands back in gassho in front of your chest.

10. Repeat steps 2 to 3 for three minutes.

11. Silently say to yourself, or out loud, with meaning and purpose, seven times "This connection will go stronger with each new day, my three bodies a perfect whole will make."

12. Allow yourself to be still for a few moments and then bow to the Universe to finish.

Fig 1.7

Fig 1.8

Chapter Two

Finding Direction, Being Guided

All too often we are presented with a vast array of conflicting directions that we can take in life. In reality, there are two paths in life to choose from, a **physical** and a **spiritual** path. There may be a time when we are allowed to tentatively tip toe with a foot on each path, but at some point we have to be bold and make our decision. Which path are we going to take? Do we want to achieve spiritual fulfilment and expand our Universal awareness, *or* would we rather revel in the delights that a physically driven lifestyle has to offer? Make your choice only when you are truly ready, because **you** know that the choice is right for **you**, not because anyone has told you to do so and most certainly, not out of fear.

It follows, inevitably, that when we are more deeply connected to our spiritual selves our lives becomes far more guided. The Light that shines within shows us a path and propels us in that direction for our own good, sometimes gently, sometimes forcefully, depending on what we need at the time. We can only experience true completeness if we are following our higher path. There may be fleeting moments of exuberance and euphoria within our lives, but the real journey to happiness awaits us on our spiritual journey. This journey on earth may seem astoundingly short or depressingly long, but remember to be patient; our life on earth, on the scale of the Universe is fleeting.

By separating these paths, there is no suggestion that we may not be physically grounded. Rather, the aim is that our head lies metaphorically in heaven and our feet remain firmly planted on the ground. That way, we can act as a bridge between heaven and earth, being utterly grounded in our role on this planet and gaining wisdom from the 'heavens' or the Universe above us.

A physical path implies that we have chosen not to pursue our spirituality whatsoever, but instead lead a life driven purely by our own physical desires. This path can ultimately never lead to 'oneness,' for a truly spiritual soul is driven by their true purpose on earth and not by their earthly obsessions.

It is all well and good knowing that we would like to make positive spiritual changes in our life, but another thing altogether knowing which route to take. As I mentioned previously, we are presented with thousands of directions to take by the people around us, in reality there are only two, physical and spiritual. Remember these choices. We must be in a state of awareness in order that we may be conscious of the signs we are given by the Universe. Believe me; we are given many of them. Most people, including myself have blindly missed or misconstrued many of the signs given to them in life. I spent years missing them, until on the train journey to my Reiki course I saw a huge sign out of the window saying, 'Prepare to Meet Thy God.' At that moment I realised my life would change forever and it certainly did.

The most important thing, which I have said before and I will repeat right now, is, 'seek and you will find.' However, seek **within you** for your most vital answers. If you have a burning question just ask God. If you do not believe in God then ask the Universe. If you do not believe in either of these, then trust your inner voice. Ask and you will certainly be given direction. Never be afraid to ask questions, words were created for that very reason and never be afraid to be seeking, for those who are searching are truly blessed.

The exercises below will help you on your spiritual journey, to tap into your intuition and establish where you should be focusing your attention.

The first exercise, called Path Seeking, will help you to find direction in life, accessing your own insightfulness and allowing you to acknowledge that you are seeking your higher purpose.

The constant repetition of the affirmation will form a dedication within you to commit to establishing and fulfilling your higher purpose.

The second exercise, called Guiding Light, is to help set your spirit free from its entrapment in your physical existence. This will allow you to see 'outside the box' and reinforce the vital connection between your body, mind and soul. Once you can achieve this, you will be able to separate your physical thinking from your spiritual guidance. This in turn, will aid you in making the decisions that are most beneficial to your higher self and for your higher divine path.

By prostrating yourself in this particular technique, you are demonstrating humility in the face of a greater power and reinforcing your constant willingness to be guided.

If you practise these exercises regularly enough, you will be well on the road to knowing the truth of the Universe that is hidden from so many. Practise them diligently. Keep your eyes wide open to look for those vital signs.

Exercises

Path Seeking

1. Lie in a comfortable position either on a yoga mat, on the floor or on your bed. Place your hands behind your head cupping the base of your skull, so you are resting your head in your palms and your elbows are on the ground (Fig 2.1).

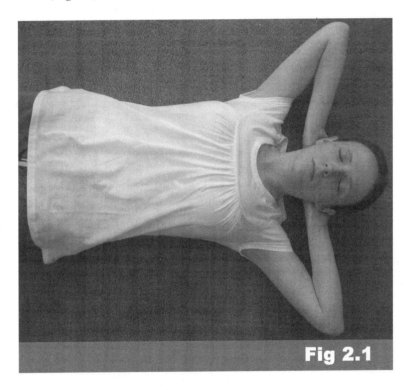

Fig 2.1

2. Breathe in through your nose, very slowly, for a count of four. Hold your breath for four, and then breathe out through your mouth, for a count of four. Hold your

breath for four and repeat the breathing process for several minutes or until you feel relaxed.

3. Close your eyes and visualise your whole body and the whole room engulfed in beautiful bright white Light. Breathe slowly and deeply without counting.

4. Silently say to yourself, or out loud, with meaning and purpose, for five to twenty minutes "I seek my higher path on earth that I may know the truth."

5. When you have finished, sit up with your back straight, place your hands in gassho (prayer position) in front of your chest and bow to the Universe, silently saying "I thank you for your eternal guidance and love."

Guiding Light

1. Sit down comfortably on the floor in seiza (on your knees with your bottom resting on your heels). Make sure your back is straight. Place your hands in gassho (prayer position) in front of your chest. Raise your palms, still in gassho straight above your head (Fig 2.2).

2. Turn your palms outwards so they face away from your body (Fig 2.3).

3. Prostrate yourself on the floor, so your knees are still bent but your body is face down with your forehead rested on the floor and your arms stretched out above your head, in an almost semi-foetal position. Have your palms resting lightly on the floor (Fig 2.4).

4. Silently say to yourself, or out loud, seven times, with meaning and purpose, "Let the Light of the Universe be my guide, so in my physical state I will not hide."

5. Raise yourself off the ground so you are upright again (Fig 2.5). Place your hands back in gassho position, arms outstretched above your head (Fig 2.6).

6. Bring your palms back down in gassho position, to your chest (Fig 2.7).

7. Silently say to yourself, or out loud, with meaning and purpose, "I connect my heart..." then move your hands in gassho to your stomach (Fig 2.8) and continue, ."..my body," then move your hands in gassho to the middle of your forehead (representing your third eye) (Fig 2.9) and continue, ."..my spirit, to fulfil Divine will on earth."

Fig 2.2

Fig 2.3

Fig 2.4

8. Repeat the entire process as many times as you like for between five and twenty-five minutes.

9. At the end of the process, bow to the Universe in gassho (prayer position) with your hands in front of your chest.

Fig 2.5 — Fig 2.6

Fig 2.7

Fig 2.8

Fig 2.9

Facing Life, Being Truth

Introduction to Part Two

"The hardest challenge in life is to face life head on, but once you accept the consequences of your actions, you can become wiser, you can move on. Let right living and right thinking carry you on your journey and you will reach the Light."

We all have to face up to our responsibilities in life, whether we like it or not. We all need to endeavour to face those responsibilities every single day in this life, or else suffer the aftermath in the next. We are here on this planet to learn lessons from our life, to take a cold hard look at what we have done and admit to our mistakes. If we can acknowledge our mistakes and have the foresight to perceive the consequences of our actions, we have the potential to be free.

Making mistakes is inevitable and if you learn from them then you will foster your spiritual growth. It is when people do not learn from their mistakes that a plethora of problems materialise and their self-development is delayed or squandered.

One of the hardest things I have had to do in this life is to face up to the blunders I have made. There is not a day that goes by, when I don't remember those errors, because learning from them has helped me to grow and help others do the very same. There are times when we all want to hide from the truth, many people spend their entire lives evading reality, but it will hit them, indeed it will hit us all one day. Harsh as this may sound, the truth is often disturbing.

Many inhabitants of the twenty-first century world are locked in a life long daydream. They may choose to exist in this dream like state, or they may sincerely believe that they are wide-awake when in reality they are totally intoxicated by the reverie that deludes them. If you shout 'wake up!' it will fall on deaf ears, your voice will be but a ghost that they cannot perceive.

These inhabitants wander around, mesmerised by the sparkle of diamonds, the allure of gold, the promise of wealth, power and reverence. Their egos longing to be massaged and caressed and desires fulfilled. Then, when they eventually fall down they become sickly, irrational and bitter. They bury their heads in the sand and cry, "oh cruel world, how could you let this happen to me. The injustice, the sadness, the tears the pain, what have I done to deserve this?"

The blame game is all too easy, because it means we can avoid taking responsibility and changing our lives. The thing is, it can never lead to happiness or self-development because whilst we are consistently passing the buck, we are neglecting our spiritual nature and damaging others paths and our own. Take responsibility for your actions. It almost sounds trite, but it's most certainly true, if you can take accountability, you can nourish your soul and become a much happier and more peaceful human being.

We should not hold God or the Universe responsible for our misery. Humanity breeds its own suffering. We have all cried "why me!" but it is up to us to take control of our own lives, to take a good hard look at ourselves and see where we went wrong. Only when we truly feel the pain of our actions, accept that pain as a blessing and a lesson in life and accept our responsibilities, only then can we realise heaven, or real 'oneness,' or 'completeness.' When you can truly look at life, understand all life and know the Universe and your place in the Universe, then you have arisen from your dream and the truth can be yours.

Truth, you may ask, "What is the truth? Is everybody's truth the same?" You can only know the truth once you have developed a higher awareness, once you can see the 'bigger picture.' When you reach this peak, the truth will become so apparent that you can no longer ignore it, no matter how hard you may try. To reach this stage, requires certain changes to take place within you and I have devised methods to help you witness these changes take place, before your very eyes. Don't see the world as it presents itself to you. See it as it *really* is.

Part Two is divided into sections, each one exploring a different goal for you to attain, with explanations of how to achieve that goal using specific exercises. You will learn to: understand and control your anger, release your worries, know your consequences, be responsible and the ultimate that naturally follows, know the truth and all that it stands for. As always, practise these exercises regularly and your life will change for the better. We have to put effort into life to get anything out of it. Short cuts are for the enlightened.

Chapter Three

Understanding Anger

We all get angry sometimes and some people get angry all the time. Most of us harbour unresolved anger from our early childhood days that accumulates as we mature into adulthood and undergo further emotional traumas. In the twenty-first century, almost everyone seems to be incensed with rage. By channelling anger in the wrong way, we can harm ourselves physically, emotionally and spiritually, disrupting our entire health and well-being.

As human beings, we tend to become terribly irritated with things we cannot change. Yes, it may be aggravating that your car is stuck in traffic and your normal commute to work has taken twice as long, but ultimately there is nothing you can do about it, other than to become agitated or simply accept the situation. We need to learn to let go of our anger, rather than letting our anger control us. This does not mean having to abandon all anger. The world is filled with many atrocious injustices that we have every right to feel aggrieved about.

There is no sense though, in pouring over it at every waking moment. Rather focus your attention on the areas where you can make a difference, change what you are able to change and accept what you cannot.

Humans are completely obsessed with having control in their lives, but the reality is that we are subject to the will of the Universe and we have very little control. It is better to be guided by the Universe. If you try to control it, you will soon be shown who's boss. Let go, be guided and be free.

We can, sometimes, have a tendency to take our anger out on the most vulnerable or perceived weak people around us. This often results in some parents taking out their anger on their children, either deliberately or subconsciously. In turn, we then end up with yet another generation of emotionally damaged, spiritually stunted individuals.

We cannot evolve spiritually if we cannot control and understand our anger. Neither can we evolve, if we repress all our anger internally because this will damage us on so many levels, not to mention the grief it will cause to those closest to us. We very often like to think of ourselves as mature, wise adults but within us all, is a screaming tantrum prone three year old who wants to get their own way. It is unwise to use our emotions to manipulate people, either through tears or aggression. Both can be incredibly powerful. Yet doing this indicates a lack of responsibility, an unwillingness to grow up and be an adult, and we all have to grow up at some point.

The key is to speak your mind, but based on intuition rather than rash judgements. If someone upsets you, deal with the situation intuitively and objectively. Take a deep breath in and express in a clear and eloquent manner what it is that concerns you, without launching into a personal, frenzied attack on the person. Aggression does not make people more inclined to see your point of view, in fact quite the opposite.

People, by virtue of human nature, become very defensive and hostile when confronted with blind rage.

If at all possible, take a step back from the situation and generate a healthy discussion spoken with uncomplicated assertiveness, you will achieve much more. This is especially so with children. Just imagine being only four feet tall, with a screaming red-faced giant gushing senseless mumbo jumbo at you. If your child misbehaves, you need to bend down to their level, look them in the eye and explain your grievances in a firm manner and in a way that they will understand.

If you have spent your entire life suppressing your emotional traumas and being passive, then it is a gigantic step to be able to truly express yourself freely in these kinds of situations. However, with time, effort and through practising the exercises in this chapter, you will be able to find the words to communicate to others how you are really feeling. When you can let go of your anger, remain calm and elevate yourself spiritually above your situation, you can start to perceive the bigger picture, the Way of the Universe.

The beauty of walking your higher path and gaining a higher level of awareness is that situations which once made you highly stressed and volatile suddenly, seem so terribly insignificant. It's as if you are a hundred feet tall and as you look down below, those angry aggressive people seem so tiny and vapid. Instead, you can see souls who are lost in limbo and troubled. Rising above it all is crucial in any situation.

If it helps, when you are in a confrontational situation with someone who is making you feel threatened, detach yourself from the situation and feel yourself rising above it. Imagine your body growing and reaching through the sky and as you look down visualise that person shrinking below you. As you look out at the sky and all the majestic birds flying by you will start to think, "Why on earth is that person creating such a fuss about nothing?"

When you can do this, you will always be able to have an inner calm that no one can shake, an inimitable faith. With your head up in the sky you will have clarity and focus, and with this, you will know exactly what to say to that angry person facing you with their violent temper. They are only trying to steal your precious energy, either on a conscious or subconscious level. Quite simply, do not allow them. If their argument requires a response, then plainly state yours and walk away. If they are merely taunting you, for their own amusement, then don't even dignify them with a response. Turn your back on them. You will be surprised how quickly certain people lose interest, when they realise they have no power over you.

People who are hungry for power over others, feed off the vulnerable. If you are strong, confident and resolute in your convictions, they will leave you alone, because you have the true power of a spiritual connection, which is far greater than any physical power they could ever possess.

Be aware of your own anger and be aware of other peoples. You may find that you can see similarities in your angry reactions and the angry reactions of those around you. Watch how their anger influences those around them. See the negative and hostile atmosphere they create and learn from it. Take responsibility for yourself. Vow to deal with your own anger in a healthy, productive way to benefit yourself and to benefit others.

Anger can be incredibly hard to shed, especially if we have a lifetime's worth stored up in our tiny earthly bodies. At some point, the root of the rage needs to be dealt with. If the cause of the anger is neglected, it will continue to accumulate and grow stronger, until it damages us as individuals or other people in our external environment.

The exercise below will help you to understand your anger, to see the true causes and to relinquish that anger for your own spiritual growth and peace of mind. The Light used in the exercise will help to draw the anger out of you, to heal you emotionally and with the affirmations to plant serenity within your soul. The hand positions used will allow you to push Universal energy into all the major organs of your body.

Practise this technique as often as you can and your energetic frequency will be elevated over time. Allow yourself to rise above it all and see the bigger picture and you will be well on the way to finding the truth.

Exercise

Understanding Anger

1. Stand with your feet hip width apart, keeping your back straight and your arms relaxed by your side. Keep your shoulders down and relaxed (Fig 3.1). Stand like this for about thirty seconds.

2. Place your hands gently in gassho (prayer position) in front of your chest. Breathe in very slowly and deeply, through your nose and breathe out through your mouth.

3. Visualise a bright white Light, so bright it is almost impossible to look at, coming down through space as far up as the eye can see. See the Light enter the crown of your head from above, like a radiant beam and allow the Light to permeate your entire body from your head through to the tips of your toes.

4. As you breathe in and out allow the Light to draw your spiritual body up taller, so your head touches the ceiling.

5. Move your hands gently apart, palms facing each other, so there is about a football sized space between your hands (Fig 3.2).

6. As you breathe in and out allow the Light beam to travel down your neck, into your shoulders, along your arms and out of your hands.

7. Visualise and feel the Light travelling back and forth between your palms, as you continue to breathe very slowly and deeply. Continue this process for between

three and fifteen minutes, allowing the energy between your palms to build up and gain strength.

8. Cover your eyes with your palms (Fig 3.3) and feel the intense heat and Light from your palms radiate into your head.

9. Silently say to yourself, or out loud, with meaning and purpose, seven times, "Light of the Universe, allow me to see the true meaning of the anger that resides within me. Light of the Universe, allow me to let go, of all the anger that damages me, so that I may grow." As you say these words, forcefully push the affirmation through your eyes and into the centre of your head.

10. Place your palms at the side of your head, with your palms covering your temples (Fig 3.4). Feel the Light continue to radiate into your head and repeat again silently or out loud seven times, the affirmation from step 9. As you say these words, push the affirmation through your temples and into your head.

11. Place your hands over the back of your head, with your palms cupping the base of your skull (Fig 3.5). Feel the Light push through into the base of your brain. Repeat the affirmation seven times, as in step 9, again pushing the affirmation into the base of your brain.

12. Cup your throat with the palms of your hands (Fig 3.6). Feel the Light permeate through your neck. Repeat the affirmation seven times, as in step 9, pushing the affirmation into your neck.

13. Place your hands, on either side, at the top of your chest (Fig 3.7). Repeat the affirmation seven times as in step 9, pushing the affirmation into your stomach.

14. Place your hands, on either side, at the bottom of your chest (Fig 3.8). Repeat the affirmation seven times as in step 9, pushing the affirmation into your stomach

15. Place your hands over your abdomen (Fig 3.9). Repeat the affirmation seven times as in step 9, pushing the affirmation into your stomach.

Fig 3.1

Fig 3.2

Fig 3.3

Fig 3.4 Fig 3.5 Fig 3.6

16. Place your hands just below your navel on either side, over your pelvic region (Fig 3.10). Feel the Light flood into your tanden (3 cm below the navel). Repeat the affirmation seven times as in step 9, forcefully pushing the affirmation into your tanden and pelvic region.

17. Take five deep breaths in and out, breathing in through your nose and out through your mouth and return your hands to gassho (prayer position) in front of your chest.

18. Allow yourself to be still for a few moments and then bow to the Universe to finish.

Fig 3.7   Fig 3.8

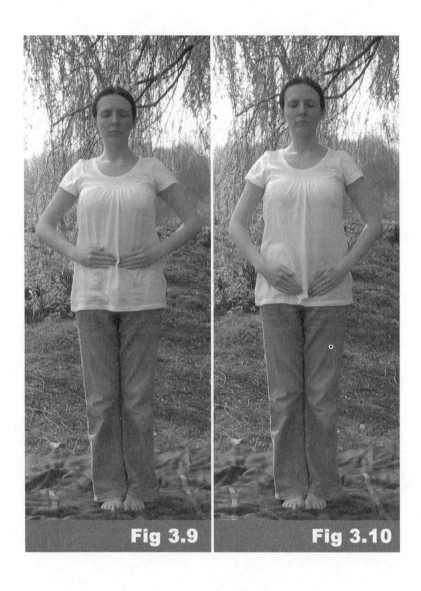

Fig 3.9   Fig 3.10

Chapter Four

Lifting Worry

Worry is conditioned into us from an early age and seems to spread like some kind of plague. Our daily conversations with friends, family, work colleagues and others, pass from person to person, breeding a new topic to agonise over. The daily grind we encounter allows multitudes of thoughts to play over in our minds, on a never-ending loop, until we eventually develop insomnia, chronic stress, digestive problems and an array of other illnesses.

In fact, swiftly after our abrupt departure from our mothers' wombs we start building anxieties. We worry about being fed, being away from our parents, going to school, gaining approval from our parents and peers, succeeding at school. As we become older, we turn our attention to worrying about: finding jobs, keeping jobs, forming relationships, job promotions, moving house, commuting, driving, shopping, developing illnesses, having children. I could go on and on for an aeon.

We are caught up in a constant daily struggle, trapped inside a tiny box where all we can manage to do is run back and forth, back and forth, frustrated like caged animals. We never stop to be in the moment, our minds are always racing ahead to the next activity and we are worrying about that activity, even before the previous one has been completed. There never seems to be the time to stop and take stock. Even if there is plenty of time, many people do not grasp the opportunity to use it judiciously. They don't want to stop, even for a second. They are scared that if they do, their life will never be the same again. They will have to ponder on their life's choices and this, they fear, could ultimately lead to depression, or worse, the need to take risks.

A friend of mine once said to me, after she had parted ways with her partner that she couldn't possibly spend a night staying in the house contemplating, because this would cause her to think too much. Thinking, it would seem, is a daunting prospect.

This is the irony of the situation many of us, in the Western world, are in. We are like cogs in a wheel, constantly perpetuating the same motion, yet we kind of like the routine of the wheel, it is a nice safe option. We are worried that if we get off the wheel, we will question our entire existence or else cease to exist at all.

A work colleague of mine once proclaimed to me, that he didn't want to consider that he might have a spiritual nature, because this would bring up too many questions about the Universe that he simply could not answer. The real fear was that he might have to question his actions. However people try to dress it up, humanity is wracked with fear and worry, the mutual comrades that feed off each others ability to draw people away from their true purpose in life.

The whole scenario sounds utterly ludicrous, we are meant to be the highly 'liberated' individuals of the developed

Western world, the advanced children of the twenty-first century. We have gadgets for almost anything and everything you could ever possibly want them for. Sure, society has developed technologically, we know how to make money, accumulate possessions, promote products and build fantastic machines, but we have largely lost touch with our spirituality.

For all the things we have, all the money, all the consumer goods and all the choices that a developed world has to offer, for all these things and more, we have a ceaseless abundance of troubles and woe. We have the 'poor me' syndrome. "Woe is me, I have to work twelve hours a day in a job I hate to pay for my £500,000 house, my wide screen television, my laptop, my mobile phone camera, my computer, my DVD, my Blackberry, my car." It's as if we feel that without our collection of gadgets, we will be desolate and worthless. We have lost sight of the little things that matter and are lost in our little boxes with our big commodities that serve as our main form of escapism. Yet, all we need to do is to open the lid of the box, climb out and see the bigger picture. Then we can say, "Wow, I'm glad I am not a cog anymore!" We have a choice. We just have to make it.

To let go of worry, to not get bogged down with our busy daily existence, we need to find our true paths in life. Once we surrender to our paths, everything will fall into place. The worry will seep away, because we are fulfilling our ultimate purposes. As our awareness expands, we no longer feel like we are caught up in the stresses of our lives, but instead we have faith in the Universe that everything will be fine. We have an inner knowing that no man can break, we are lead by inner guidance and we seek our answers from **within**.

The reason we have established this immovable faith, is because we know we are doing the right things to nourish our soul, we know that we can move mountains. Faith and worry do not complement each other, because to worry too much is to demonstrate a lack of faith. If we lack faith it stalls our spiritual progress, halts our journey to enlightenment and ultimate freedom.

The desire to shed our worries is an easy task, but actually being able to do it is infinitely harder. We are so damn good at worrying. We are so used to it. You might even say it's what we excel the most at. The amazing thing about re-connecting with your higher self and relying always on your intuition is that worry becomes a great deal easier to shift because your life is more guided, you have direction and you have greater wisdom. You will realise, "hey this is what I am here for, I am great at this and I enjoy it too. What was I worrying about in the first place?" You will learn to appreciate the real beauty that exists in the Universe and gain satisfaction from this realisation. On your beautiful passage to freedom, the exercises I have crafted below will assist you in making worry a thing of the past.

The first exercise is called Worry Shifter, and uses meditation (a powerful worry releaser) and affirmation to build up your faith and allow your insignificant worries to be well and truly buried. It will foster within you trust in the Universe to be your guide. By using this exercise regularly, you will strengthen your connection to your higher self and replace worry in your head, heart and body, with focus, clarity and a sense of peace.

Drawing your hands down your body in this exercise is utilised to cleanse and purify yourself and holding your feet will help to ground and centre you. The little insignificant, needless worries will be buried and dispersed, whilst Light is lifted over you, so that you can foster faith in yourself and the Universe. As with all the techniques in this book, this will take time, continued effort and a great deal of practise.

The second technique is a very intuitive method for problem solving. Sometimes, when you are overburdened in life, it can help you to gain clearer vision if you can assess where the most problematic areas of your life are and in turn find an appropriate way to address them. This is achieved through producing a list to establish the main problem areas in your work, home and social life. Then, utilising your intuition, you will choose which one(s) need to be addressed first.

Following this procedure, you will open yourself up to the Universe and ask for guidance on how to solve the specific problem(s). Either instantly, or within three days you will have your answer. Accept the first answer that comes to you. Don't try to solve everything at once though, deal with one thing at a time and you will experience greater results. Only perform this particular technique, once you have spent at least several weeks or more practising some of the other meditation exercises twice daily, so you get used to accepting guidance and understanding your intuition.

Exercises

Worry Shifter

1. Sit down comfortably on the floor or on a chair in agura (cross-legged). Make sure your back is straight. Place your hands in gassho (prayer position) in front of your chest. Remain seated in this position for several minutes, breathing very slowly and deeply (through your nose) and staying focused on the feeling of the passage of the air in and out of your nostrils.

2. When you feel more relaxed, place your palms over your eyes (Fig 4.1) for several seconds. Following this, gently draw your palms over your face (Fig 4.2) and the sides of your throat (Fig 4.3), drawing your hands palms facing down, over your chest (Fig 4.4), down over your stomach (Fig 4.5), along your thighs (Fig 4.6), over your knees along your ankles and feet. When you reach your toes, hold them with your hands for a few seconds. (Fig 4.7).

3. Place your palms on the floor, on either side of your body and silently say to yourself, or out loud, with meaning and purpose, seven times, "I bury the worries that are truly insignificant. I let the Light of the Universe be my guide."

4. As you say these words, breathe out slowly through your nose and feel all the niggling minor worries you have, being drawn through your body, entering your arms and being isolated in the palms of your hands. Using visualisation, forcefully push all those worries into the ground. Feel them go deeper and deeper into the ground until they vanish from your palms.

Fig 4.1

Fig 4.2

Fig 4.3

Fig 4.4

Fig 4.5

Fig 4.6

Fig 4.7

Fig 4.8

5. Turn your palms to face upwards on the ground (Fig 4.8), then raise them in a semi-circle above your body (Fig 4.9), drawing up energy as white Light around you until your palms meet in gassho (prayer position) above your head. Visualise yourself surrounded by a semi-circle of Light.

6. Bring your palms down to rest, still in gassho, on the crown of your head (Fig 4.10).

7. Silently say to yourself, or out loud, seven times, "I trust in the Universe and my higher self to guide me through my life. Let faith replace worry in my head."

8. Once you have completed this bring your palms, still in gassho to the front of your chest and repeat silently, or out loud, seven times, "I trust in the Universe and my higher self to guide me through my life. Let faith replace worry in my heart."

9. Bring your hands still in gassho to your tanden (3cm below your navel) (4.11) and repeat silently, or out loud, seven times, "I trust in the Universe and my higher self, to guide me through my life. Let faith replace worry in my body."

10. Place your hands in gassho, back in front of your chest and spend a couple of minutes basking in the Light surrounding you.

11. When you have finished, bow to the Universe.

Fig 4.9

Fig 4.10

Fig 4.11

Problem Solving

1. Grab a sheet or two of A4 paper and a pen. Draw a table divided into four columns and leave yourself plenty of rows. Head each column as follows: Home Life, Work Life, Social Life and Spiritual Needs.

2. Under each column write a list of all your problems that fit into that category. Each section can include anything to do with that aspect of your life such as: relationships with your partner and children, bills to pay at home and financial worries in the Home Life section, relationships with work colleagues and prioritising work load in the Work Life section etc.

Example

Home Life	Work Life	Social Life	Spiritual Needs
No time to myself	Boss expects too much from me	Feel obliged to go out when I am too tired	Feel like a part of me is missing
Too much housework to do..no time	Hate my job	Some friends seem to be using me	Find it hard to make sense of the world
Can't afford to pay the bills	Don't feel motivated		
Not enough time with my partner	Negative relationship with one of my work colleagues	Feel lonely even in a crowd	Difficult to understand myself
Can't sleep at night	Not earning enough	Feel left out of everything when out with friends	Feel lost
			Lacking direction

3. Once you have listed everything you can possibly think of, find a quiet place to sit down, either on a chair or the floor. Take a slow, deep breath in and out and place your palms over your eyes. Silently say to yourself, or out loud, with meaning and purpose, "Light of the Universe let me see, which problem is my first priority."

4. Sit quietly as you breathe in and out slowly for several minutes, remaining with your palms over your eyes. Don't try to control your thoughts just let them enter your mind and then drift away again.

5. When you feel calmer, take your hands away from your eyes and grab your pen. Look at the table you have drawn and without even thinking, straight away put a star by the problem that you feel intuitively drawn to. It does not matter what section it is in, the divisions are just to help you naturally see where most of the problems reside. This will naturally assist you in solving these dilemmas.

6. Again sit quietly, breathing slowly, with your palms over your eyes for a few minutes. Silently say to yourself, or out loud, "Light of the Universe let me see how I may solve this problem I have before me." Following this, repeat silently to yourself or out loud what the problem is.

7. Remain sitting quietly, with your hands covering your eyes, for between five and fifteen minutes. The answer may pop into your head instantly, or if not, you should receive your answer from the Universe within the following three days. The answer will either come to you as intuition (so you will just know what you have to do),

or as a sign, or as a vision. You should accept the first answer you are given, as this is your intuition.

8. You can repeat steps 3-6 for about three or four of your problems at a time if you wish, prioritising each problem accordingly. However, I would suggest that you address one issue first and find the answer to that and then move onto the next one. If you try to fix too many things at once, you will end up missing all the signs and getting frustrated. If you tackle each one in turn, you will have the satisfaction of ticking each problem off in turn and empowering yourself to take control of your situation.

9. When you have completed the technique. Place your hands in gassho (prayer position) in front of your chest and bow to the Universe.

(N.B. You don't have to restrict yourself to one column at a time. Work intuitively, the problems are likely to be interconnected and you may have to address problems over several columns to make real headway.)

Chapter Five

Being Thankful

Accepting our many blessings in life is one of the most critical things we can do. People sometimes have a tendency to ignore the beauty of life and dwell too much on their own misgivings and the prevalent negativity surrounding them. When we can come to accept that we are truly blessed we can learn quickly to become much more contented individuals. This of course means being truly thankful for all the 'wonderful' events that take place in our lives, but much more than this, it means being sincerely and most humbly grateful for all the pain we experience. For once, we can wholeheartedly perceive that our pain is in reality a most precious blessing, we can then learn and progress as spiritual beings.

From our human perspective some of our pain may seem entirely unbearable, it may bring us crippling sadness and lead us to question the very essence of our beliefs. We may feel utterly wretched and plunge onto our knees, with the intolerable anguish besieging our hearts. If, however, we can see past the initial pain to a valuable lesson and to an amazing opportunity for spiritual development, then we have done much to set ourselves free. This requires more than simply sounding out the words. We have to truly mean those words from the bottom of our hearts. The gratitude must be entirely genuine. There is great futility in trying to fool the Universe or ourselves, with either devious or half felt words. Each of our thoughts creates a corresponding energy, whether helpful or harmful, and creates a consequence for us or for those around us. Thus, we must endeavour to be true to ourselves and not create a situation of denial. Our souls know us completely.

We must be aware, of course that pain is a term we have coined for suffering and we associate that term with what we perceive to be the negative situations in our life. Those circumstances, we often feel, take away from our true happiness in life, but the reality is, that quite to the contrary, those events are incredibly constructive. On a Universal level the word pain does not generate quite the same connotations.

Everything in this Universe has a very distinct purpose that may be hidden from us, at the time, or indeed all of the time. We are often being shown a new direction to facilitate our heightened strength, determination and courage of our physical, emotional and spiritual bodies. Genially, we are invited to change our lives for the better. If we embrace this opportunity, the journey to freedom will unfold before us. Should we refuse to take heed of this important instruction, we will repeatedly be presented with similar situations, until we finally demonstrate a sincere willingness to learn.

Think of a very young child, every day witnessing the actions of their parents and attentively observing, absorbing and mimicking their behaviour. Supposing that parent leaves the child without any boundaries and portrays an image of nonchalance and passivity. All hell may reign. The child may believe that no responsibility is required in life, that there is nothing to learn, for all who surround them will submit to their demands.

As adulthood prevails, the individual will most likely have retained those early values and could potentially walk though their entire life without learning a single lesson and without appreciation for anyone or anything that does not serve their whims. Conversely, had that very same child been brought up by their parents with true approval, unconditional love and healthy boundaries and discipline, they would be more liable to grow up truly valuing life and what is stands for. They would truly comprehend and learn from all their experiences, because they were shown by their parents that sometimes the most priceless lessons are extremely hard for us to take. Realisation would then hopefully set in for them, that it was all completely worth the testing time.

Following on from this example, we are children of the Universe or of God and sometimes we have to be presented with trying situations so that we too may become wise adults.

All too often we see our mistakes with hindsight, the key though, is to have foresight enough not to make them in the first place. So be truly thankful and humble and you will never cease to grow. Then enlightenment can one day be yours.

The technique below, entitled Grateful Living, will enable you to expel negative thoughts and emotions from your being, replacing that negativity with absolute humility and gratitude. By gently smiling to yourself, you can realise all that you have to be thankful for. With the affirmation, you can honestly give thanks for every event in your life, whether you deem those occasions to be joyful or otherwise. Light will replace the dark, negative energy and emotions, as you breathe these out from your body and allow the Universe to convert that dark energy to positive Light.

As you become more intuitive through this exercise, challenging situations will seem less insurmountable because you will have the awareness to look at your life in a more objective way. Hindsight will be accompanied by foresight.

Practise this exercise at least once a day and alongside this, make a mental note to yourself to try and place a more positive slant on some of the more challenging situations in your life. In other words, see clearly beyond the actual event, to the wisdom you are meant to have gleaned from it.

Exercise

Grateful Living

1. Sit down comfortably, either on the floor in seiza (on your knees with your bottom resting on your heels) or in agura (cross-legged) or on a chair. Make sure your back is straight. Place your hands in gassho (prayer position) in front of your chest.

2. Breathe in through your nose slowly and deeply. As you do this, visualise white Light from above you, as far up as the eye can see, entering the crown of your head and shooting like a beam through your body, all the way into the ground as far down as the eye can see. So in effect, you have a rod of Light running throughout your body.

3. Breathe out slowly through your mouth and allow this beam of pure white Light to expand widthways through and then outside of your body, so you are sitting inside a huge beam of white Light.

4. Smile gently, just raising the corners of your mouth and focus your attention on your two middle fingers, feeling them pressed lightly against each other. Concentrate on all the sensations this brings, whilst retaining focus on the Light within and surrounding you.

5. Silently say to yourself, or out loud, twenty-one times, with meaning and purpose, "I am grateful for all the lessons I have learned. I am grateful for the pain; it was a blessing I earned."

6. Take a long, deep breath in through your nose, breathing in the beautiful white Light around you. As you breathe out through your mouth, push the dark negative energy out from your body, visualising black negative areas dislodging from your body and pouring out of your mouth.

7. Breathe in and replace the dark areas with the pure white Light around you, then silently say to yourself, or out loud, seven times, "I pray that the Universe may convert this negative energy to positive Light."

8. Repeat steps 4 through to 7 as many times as you like for up to forty minutes.

9. When you have finished, bow to the Universe.

Chapter Six

Taking Responsibility

We cannot escape the consequences of our actions. Everybody, at some point in their existence, would like to think that they could walk any path without any repercussions. I hold my hands up to admit that I have behaved atrociously in my past, in certain situations and have not given a second, or even indeed a first thought, for the consequences of my erratic, irrational behaviour. I know that I am not alone in this. There are millions, upon millions of people out there, with a deeply ingrained belief that they can do whatever they please without negative consequences. It is not uncommon for teenagers to present this sort of behaviour during puerile rebellious phases. What is more worrying though, is that there are an ever increasing number of adults who voyage through life either ignorant of, or deliberately disregarding, their responsibilities.

The twenty-first century world runs on survival of the fittest. Those who fall below the line have to clamber their way up, gripping on for dear life or else be left lagging behind in a swamp of appalling human suffering, and a complete lack of compassion. We are weary, flagging carthorses equipped with blinkers, trotting hoof after hoof along the same stretch of open road, whilst our rears are mercilessly whipped lest we should dare to turn our heads and see what envelops us like a thick gloomy fog. If only we had the wisdom to see that we can run the cart out of town, shake off our blinkered vision and gallop for the hills, to look out over the world and bear witness to and hear and shriek the truth, so that it may echo incessantly through the earth. We all have eyes to see, ears to listen and mouths to furnish the world with the Light of pure veracious insight. Yet, ignoble we cower from the truth for fear that it may set us free. We shun responsibility to live so perilously.

Surely, it is much better to act now and deal with the consequences as they arrive, rather than becoming prone to apathetic inaction and reaping the consequences that await us. If we continually act with disregard for our behaviour, then we affect ever greater numbers of those around us, building consequence after consequence until we reap a dose of our own bitter medicine. Some people might sincerely believe that the consequences of their actions will never catch up with them, but this could not be further from the truth. If the scales are tipped one way, something will tip them back the other.

Seeing the consequences and taking responsibility is a huge part of our quest for facing reality and being truthful. They must be united in harmonious bliss. There is no point being aware of the consequences, but ignoring them anyway. This is truthfully much worse, for when one is ignorant the consequences are unknown and thus blame cannot be so readily apportioned. When one knows the very consequences, yet still chooses to overlook them the outcome will naturally be much worse. Most of us know, deep down *anyway*, what the results of our actions will be. Some would rather just not face up to it, in pretence of not knowing any better. No one can hide from the truth forever.

When we are children, it is up to our parents to teach us responsibility and we cannot be blamed for the sufferings we endure from our parents or those around us. Once we have grown into adults though, there comes a point when we all know, deep within the inner realms of our being, the distinct difference between right and wrong. This is not because of any morality bred into us by our culture, environment or the values of our parents, but an inherent wisdom that inhabits our souls. There is an innate understanding of the laws of the Universe. Denial of this can lead to years of accumulated guilt and harsh judgements that we hurl indignantly at ourselves. The simplicity of it is that we need to just let go of our guilt and take responsibility for our actions, because ultimately, no one else is going to do that for us.

So, I implore you to be conscious of the way you live your life, without self-reproach. There is really no need to punish ourselves for our past actions and failings, just to learn from these lessons, know the consequences, to be accountable and gracefully move on.

The exercises below will help you to submit to your inner knowledge, allowing you to be filled with inner calm. Once you are submerged in this state of tranquillity, you will be able to witness the consequences of the actions you have taken throughout your life.

The first technique, entitled Seeing Consequences will help to bolster your intuitive connection and through your emotions (chest) and physical body (stomach), will enable you to witness the effects of the choices you have made in life. The Universe will be your guide. Your body, mind and soul will unite so that you are able to see your true spiritual self and be that spiritual being.

The second exercise, called Taking Responsibility will help you to recognise the choices you have made in life, to accept where you are right now and truly develop spiritually, fulfilling even more of your latent inner potential. By focusing on your crown and forehead and admitting liability, you can cultivate an inner acceptance to enhance your well-being and self-development. The other areas of focus, in this technique, will help you to establish an unbreakable bond between your physical, emotional and spiritual bodies.

The affirmation will help you to acknowledge all the consequences of your actions and truly learn from these. It can be scary to look at the stark consequences of all our actions, but it is far more spiritually rewarding in the long run. If we cannot see consequences, we are in danger of acting against our intuition. When we can perceive the consequences and we change our actions for the better because of it, we develop a higher state of awareness and become more compassionate and loving human beings. This allows us to create happier and more welcome consequences for ourselves. I personally feel that Western 'civilisation' especially, has over the years bred a largely profligate society. One of the major ways of turning back the tide, even if it is only a slight improvement, is for each of us, as individuals, to pay close attention to our actions and to think incredibly carefully about the final upshot of our behaviour before we act.

Practise the two techniques in this chapter, together, at least three or four times a week, to see long term results. If you are prepared to graft for spiritual growth, you have the power to achieve great things. If you are on the hunt for overnight miracles to occur, you may forget the value of the process that gets you to where you need to be. Take things as slowly as you need to, or as fast as you need to and view each and every step as a precious footprint on your journey towards freedom.

Exercises

Seeing Consequences

1. Sit down comfortably either on the floor in seiza (on your knees with your bottom resting on your heels) or in agura (cross-legged) or on a chair. Make sure your back is straight. Place your left palm at the back of your head, over the base of your skull and place your right palm over your forehead (Fig 6.1). Breathe slowly and deeply. Remain like this for three minutes.

2. Place your right hand on the centre of your chest, at the top (Fig 6.2). Again, remain like this, breathing slowly and deeply, for three minutes.

3. Place your right hand over your stomach (covering your navel) (Fig 6.3) and remain like this for three minutes.

4. Place your right hand back on your forehead, visualising a white beam of Light coming from above you, as far as the eye can see and gently entering the top of your head. Visualise that Light filling your entire head.

5. Silently say to yourself, or out loud, with meaning and purpose, seven times, "May the Universe let me see the consequences of all my actions that I may learn from these." Maintain the visualisation of your head filled with Light as you do this.

6. Place your right hand on the centre of your chest and visualise the white Light continuing down from your head and into your chest. See the Light fill your heart, your lungs and your whole upper body from the chest upwards.

Fig 6.1

Fig 6.2

7. Repeat to yourself silently, with meaning and purpose, seven times, the affirmation from step 5.

8. Place your right hand on your stomach (over your navel) again and visualise the white Light stretching down into your stomach and below your navel, filling your lower body. Then push this Light down your legs to the tips of your toes.

9. Repeat to yourself silently, with meaning and purpose, seven times, the affirmation from step 5.

10. Place your hands in gassho (prayer position) in front of your chest and silently say to yourself, or out loud with meaning and purpose "Let the Universe unite my body, mind and soul that I may see the life in me, that I may be whole."

11. Bow to the Universe and silently say, with meaning and purpose, "I give thanks to the Light of the Universe for all the guidance and love that has been brought upon me."

Fig 6.3

Taking Responsibility

1. Sit down comfortably either on the floor in seiza (on your knees with your bottom resting on your heels) or in agura (cross-legged) or on a chair. Make sure your back is straight. Place your hands in gassho (prayer position) in front of your chest.

2. Breathe in slowly and deeply, through your nose and breathe out through your mouth. Spend several minutes focusing all your attention on the crown of your head.

3. Still focusing on the crown of your head, silently say to yourself, or out loud, with meaning and purpose, seven times, "I take responsibility for the choices I have made, I created my path and I accept what I have become."

4. Focusing your attention on the middle of your forehead (third eye), repeat seven times the same affirmation.

5. Focusing your attention on the centre of your chest, repeat the same affirmation seven times.

6. Focusing your attention on your navel area, repeat the same affirmation seven times.

7. Focusing your attention on your tanden (3cm below your navel), repeat the same affirmation seven times.

8. Place your left palm over the top of your chest in the centre and place your right palm over your navel area (Fig 6.4). Breathe slowly and deeply and remain seated like this for between two and five minutes.

9. Silently say to yourself, or out loud, with meaning and purpose, seven times, "I accept the consequences that I have created, that I may grow from these lessons and truly live by the Light."

10. Place your hands in gassho (prayer position) in front of your chest and tilt your head upwards to look above you (Fig 6.5). Silently say to yourself, or out loud, with meaning and purpose, seven times, "Let the Light of the Universe always guide me in all my responsibilities."

11. When you have finished, bow to the Universe and silently say with meaning and purpose, "I give thanks to the Light of the Universe for all that I have learned and continue to learn."

Fig 6.4

Fig 6.5

Chapter Seven

Knowing The Truth

By facing up to your life as it stands completely, witnessing all that happens to you and all that happens around you and by consciously seeing what is *really* there, rather than purely what you hope would be there, you can know the profound truth. This whole section has been devoted to helping you establish precisely what the truth is. It can seem like an elusive concept but the truth can be discovered and known to anyone who embraces their soul and personal spiritual journey. When you can thoroughly understand your anger, release your worry, be truly grateful, see the consequences of your actions and take responsibility, then you stand a very good chance of being in a place where truth stares at you boldly in the face.

There is no use in trying to know the truth, when you are not in a position to distinguish between fact and fiction. So work meticulously on all the other techniques in this section, before you come to practise the exercise in this chapter. When you are ready, you will not need to ask yourself if you know the truth, because as you look around you at your life, at the world, you will feel as if a huge veil has been lifted from your face, a veil that painted perfection on a tainted picture. Your mind will register, "oh my goodness, so this is how it really is." Henceforth, your mission in life should be to heal yourself so completely that you can speak the truth, feel the truth and be the truth always.

Sometimes it can feel like each of us is living in a box. We craft and inhabit our boxes both through our own choices and the choices of others. We punish ourselves because we cannot see outside of our boxes but we forget that our vision is obscured by the brown walls. We try to find the truth within what we already know, but the truth is most certainly not within our cardboard comfort zones. The only way to find the truth is to break down the walls, throw off the lids and absorb the glory of the Universe surrounding our tiny boxes. Then we realise that what we thought was the real truth, was based on very limited knowledge. In turn, we then discover the truth that is based on acute awareness of our intuition, our souls, the Universe and the life that exists outside of our manmade boxes.

It is vital not to be afraid of the truth, or shy away from it, because there is exquisite beauty in knowing the truth. Sometimes it is depressingly sombre, at other times it is like a spectacular rainbow on a rainy day. As your awareness and spirituality unfolds, you will hold the truth so dear to you, so close to your heart and you will never let it escape you. It may be a cliché, but the truth really will set you free.

To access the truth, delve into the core of situations in your life. Cast your eyes distantly beyond the surface of what you immediately perceive and ask yourself, "What does this situation *really* mean? What are the real implications of this occurrence?" Try not to trust people's words just because they present them with confidence, arrogance or beguiling charm.

Trust your intuition implicitly. If someone makes you feel desperately uncomfortable the very instant you enter their presence, it could be for one of two reasons. If they are a very spiritually evolved and aware individual, the uneasiness may signify your own emotional feelings of inadequacy about the way you are currently living your life, or you might feel that you are being judged. There is no need to feel this way and as you develop spiritually you will gain much more confidence. Those who have spiritual awareness, in effect, hold a mirror up to the world and the world recoils because it does not like what it sees. As we evolve spiritually ourselves, we become that mirror and present the opportunity for positive change.

Alternatively, if the person is creating an unsavoury and awkward atmosphere because you are sensing something more ominous from them, then your intuition is encouraging you to beware and tread very carefully. Your intuition is never mistaken. Always let it guide you. See beyond the words, the apparent intelligence and the eloquent language spoken with true conviction. See the motives rather than the presentation and see the soul rather than the body.

Avoid being manipulated by people. It is irrelevant if someone is older than you, or earning a higher salary than you, or if they have a greater IQ than you. Real intelligence comes from possessing true wisdom, from knowing the truth. In terms of the journey of your soul, it is your thoughts and actions that are important. Your material and physical status is irrelevant in terms of your spiritual connection and wisdom. Material wealth, a well paid job, respect from your peers and work colleagues, may seem intrinsic, but if you are without a soul connection, it is vapid and worthless.

Never let appearances deceive you. Focus beyond the images and words you are presented with, because in so many cases, the real truth of the matter is a far cry from the images being projected. This applies to yourself, to close family, to friends, to work colleagues, to powerful world figures and to all the people in the world around you. Ask yourself, "What are the real motives behind these actions?" Only place your respect and trust where it is due. Of course, there is no need to assume that everyone has an ulterior motive, but some people do and it is essential to be aware of this, for your own self-protection and spiritual development. If you are confident, strong, objective and intuitive, you will be less likely to fall foul of shysters.

When you come into realisation of the truth, you will be shocked but simultaneously in wonderment. The truth can bring sorrow as well as rapture. With great knowledge comes great responsibility, so always endeavour to use your insights judiciously. Once you see the truth you may feel somewhat aggrieved that you cannot change it, but remember that you can make footprints in the sand and that is all the Universe can ask of you.

The exercise below, entitled Facing Reality, is designed to open your mind to the reality that lies before you. You will allow radiant Light to enter your body, submerge yourself in the beauty of truth and submit yourself to your own inner wisdom and Universal guidance. In addition, this technique will stimulate your third eye, in order to allow your intuition and whatever spiritual gifts you may have to gently awaken, at a time that is right for you.

With the affirmation used, you are totally committing to seeing the truth by forcing those words into your conscious and subconscious mind. The white waterfall of Light, in this exercise, is intended to cleanse you spiritually and open you up to your own inner Light. You will be astonished, both by all the beauty that you had missed before and all pain that you ignored.

This exercise needs to be practised regularly, at least once a day for you to really feel the benefits.

Exercise

Facing Reality

1. Lie in a comfortable position either on a yoga mat, on the floor or on your bed.

2. Visualise Light cascading down from above you, like a giant powerful waterfall filling your body with beautiful pure white Light. Visualise the Light lapping over your whole body and allow your entire being to be immersed in the Light.

3. As you breathe in slowly through your nose, see and feel the Light enter your nostrils and radiate through your head. As you continue to breathe in, allow this Light to fill your lungs and stomach. As you breathe out slowly through your nose, push the Light into your arms, to the tips of your fingers and into your legs to the tips of your toes. Visualise and feel your body in its entirety wallowing in blissful Light. Maintain this visualisation for between five and twenty minutes.

4. Place your left palm over the middle of your forehead (third eye area) with your hand vertical, fingers pointing upwards. Place you right hand at the back of your head, covering the base of your skull (Fig 7.1). Maintain the visualisation of your body immersed in Light.

5. Silently say to yourself, or out loud, with meaning and purpose, seventeen times, "I am open to seeing the truth, the reality of what lies before me. I accept my inner guidance." As you say these words, visualise that the

words are coming forth from your hands and being pushed into your third eye and the base of your skull.

6. Visualise the white cascading waterfall of Light getting bigger and brighter, until it is so bright that you can barely look at it. See this Light flowing into your crown along your neck and shoulders, down your arms and out of your hands, into your third eye and the base of your skull. Your head should be completely submerged in wonderful pure white Light.

7. Visualise the affirmation from step 5 floating around in your head, along with the beautiful Light. Silently say to yourself, or out loud, with meaning and purpose, seven times, "I open myself up to the Light of the Universe for I can only be true in the face of such beauty."

8. Allow this affirmation to float around within the Light in your head, with the other affirmation. Let these affirmations expand and fill your entire body. Let calm, peace, serenity and faith in the Universe and yourself wash over you. Enjoy this feeling for as long as you like.

9. Place your arms down by your sides and gently wiggle your toes and fingers to allow yourself to come back to the room.

10. Whenever you are ready, bring yourself into a seated position, either in agura (cross-legged) or in seiza (on your knees with your bottom resting on your feet) and bow to the Universe.

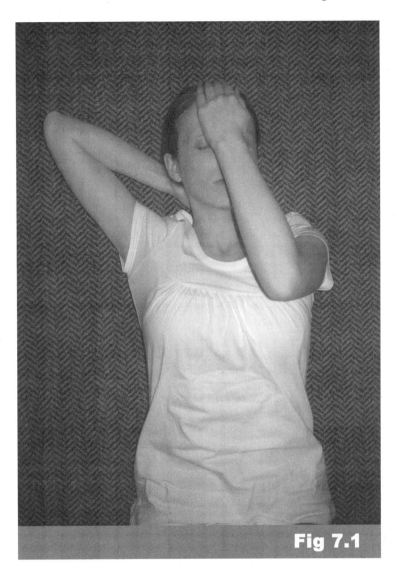

Fig 7.1

Self Healing, Self Love

Introduction to Part Three

"Our truest nature deserves to be loved from deep within. The Light that glows within us all, let it burn so bright and love that Light, for it will bestow upon you so much perfect wisdom."

Self-healing is essential to our well-being and spiritual growth. Before we even think about anyone else we need to be deeply, consciously and lovingly healing ourselves. We should always endeavour to love ourselves more than anyone else, not in an arrogant way, but in a reverential, caring, benevolent manner. Treat yourself as a precious, exquisite rare jewel. Nurture your body, mind and soul. Feel warmth and intense compassion for yourself.

Unfortunately, so many people are treading this planet consumed with inner loathing, taking their frustrations out on everyone else, not because they hate the people around them but because they passionately abhor themselves. They angrily thud from one daily task to the next, either hurling accusations at others or passively cowering in a corner afraid that someone might notice they are there.

After an exasperating, exhausting day at work, they return home, switch on the television, and engross themselves in imaginary lifestyles, yearning for the images they see to be a piece of their own reality. They wish desperately, that they had more to show for their lives, but if they stop and languish over it, it could be perceived as vulnerability. Instead, they put up with their lot and disregard their own well-being, staring grimly into the mirror, almost repulsed by the lives they feel they have lost, by the embedded lines in their tired faces.

The vicious cycle persists and if it continues without redress, their guilt and self-revulsion can cause them to drift further and further away from their spiritual path and their true higher self. They are propelled into irresponsible, risky and hedonistic behaviour, which acts as a sweet saccharin to soothe their shattered self-esteem. When this loses its appeal, the search expands for more and more self-indulgent activities until they either crumble in a fit of self-destruction or receive a deafeningly unwelcome wake-up call.

This is indubitably not the case for every individual. Some human beings live profoundly connected and admirably holistic lives. They tread each step carefully, keenly observing the consequences of all their actions and the actions of those surrounding them. Their thoughts are honest and open and confidently they bound through life with a jubilant bounce in their step. They understand the meaning of unconditional love and thus they divinely love all the souls in this Universe and mostly they cherish their own, for they know that within is a beautiful being. They are not pushovers, because sometimes we have to be cruel to be kind, but they know that their caring is with detachment and they always act for the highest good.

Undoubtedly, these are two polar extremes of human behaviour, on one side the unyielding narcissist and on the other, the angelic truth bearer. You may say, "I don't fit into any of those categories!" Yet, every single one of us on this earth whether we are enlightened souls, desire driven beings or otherwise, has these elements within us and to truly love ourselves we have to learn to acknowledge them both.

This supposition does **not** mean that we should submit to our base animal instincts or try to justify bad actions, but rather that we should accept that two poles exist within us. If we don't we can never learn to wholeheartedly love ourselves. There is dark and Light within us all, we need to aspire to the Light but not be afraid of the other side that dwells within our mortal bodies. There are elements from both those poles that we require in life for strength, determination and courage and for Divine love, compassion and humility. If we can glean the appropriate doses from each hemisphere, we can gather great strength, wisdom and prolific understanding of the world and the Universe enveloping us.

This is by no means an encouragement for everyone to go and indulge in their hedonistic side, quite the opposite, but we should appreciate ourselves, accept that both dark and Light exist and grow on every level from this acceptance. This is highly preferential to beating ourselves up about everything and casting unduly harsh judgements on our behaviour. No human being on this earth has, by Universal law the right to judge someone else and we frequently judge ourselves much more ruthlessly than we judge other people.

Look within, see what you find there and let all that will assist you on your higher path in life reign, not from a selfish perspective, but from an enlightened, holistic and self-nurturing perspective. Be objective with yourself. Take a step out of the box and watch your life from above, seated high up on a cloud. By all means assess your life and the choices you have made, take responsibility for yourself, but don't blame yourself for anything that wasn't your fault to take. Admit to your mistakes, accept accountability, let go of guilt and move on. When you let go, you can love yourself. When you can love yourself, you will heal.

This chapter has been broken down into four sections to help you establish self-confidence and self-love. This in turn will facilitate the healing process within you. Releasing the Past, will help you to face up to your life and all the choices you have made and then to let go of the guilt.

Self-Acceptance will help you to appreciate where you are right here and now, to love yourself as you are and grow from the lessons you have learned in life. We often clamber for a future we haven't yet reached, tormenting ourselves for our lack of spiritual and emotional growth. This section will help you to be in the present and acknowledge how far you have come in life, just by being where you are now.

Self-expression is vital. This section will help you to express your true emotions and your true higher self to those around you, without fear of reprisal. Being able to voice your real feelings is extremely liberating and if you can do this at all times, you will feel so much freer and happier.

The final section is entitled Being Healthy and will stress the importance of nourishing our bodies. It may sound like yet another cliché, but we really should treat our bodies as temples. They are, as I have said before, transitory vessels and if we do not look after them right now they will not serve us well. An enlightened being would not be embarking on daily trips to their local fast food restaurant. It defies the very logic of conscious living. To become healthy we need to eat pure, simple, vitamin and mineral enriched foods that cleanse our bodies and allow them to function at optimum levels.

If you put the correct fuel into your body it will look after you throughout your life. Healthy of body, healthy of mind, healthy of spirit, we cannot neglect any one of these and overcompensate in the other areas. We need to possess a truly harmonious balance between all three.

Chapter Eight

Releasing The Past

Many of us desperately cling to the past with melancholic nostalgia, either musing about our lost youth wishing we were back there again to re-capture it, or pouring over all our past mistakes, longing to be able to travel back in time and make alternative choices. This unhealthy obsession with what we cannot change in life, leads to a diminishing of personal and spiritual growth.

Those individuals who pine after their lost youth are entirely forgetting the point of our existence, which is to learn and grow from our experiences. They have not yet reached a point in their lives where they are readily taking responsibility for themselves and considering the consequences of all their actions. By coveting their prior selves, they have lost their way in life and cannot possess real insight or foresight until they stop languishing over days gone by.

If all we do is look back to the past wistfully, how can we ever hope to evolve as humans and as spiritual beings? We cannot be happy or free if we are locked in a time warp. We should be able to look at where we are now, where we were in the past, and say, "you know what, I learned a lot from those experiences and this will stand me in good stead in life." We need to see opportunities for personal growth in the present and future, rather than trying to reverse the sands of time.

Those individuals who yearn to forge a different past are wasting their time and energy on trying to re-direct the course of the Universe.

There are two types of people who find themselves in this predicament, those who regret their past exploits for more spiritual reasons and those who regret it for selfish reasons. For example, if an individual once stole from an elderly lady in their youth, they may with hindsight repent, because they realise that their actions were erroneous. This would thus be a spiritual reason. If that very same person, instead, regretted their past actions because it resulted in a prison sentence for them, this would be a very selfish physical reason. The former needs to accept that their mistakes were a lesson in life, learn from those lessons, let go of their past and carry on living their life in a healthier and more conscious way. They should try to understand that their life will not necessarily be easy, but that the challenges are opportunities for personal growth.

The latter has learned very little, if anything from their existence on earth and is wallowing in their own self-pity and egoism, rather than understanding the consequences of their actions on those around them. Either they will at some point enter a period of self-realisation, where they acknowledge their responsibilities in life, or they will be continually bound into a cycle of self-destructive, remorseless behaviour. They can only plump for the selfish option up to a point, because ultimately, one day, they will be held accountable.

The guilt that many of us hold onto throughout our lives, can result in us either endeavouring to overcompensate for these feelings by constantly trying to please others, or by doing the complete opposite and misdirecting all our anger, taking it out on those around us. Both of these options are completely unhealthy for us. In addition, they distract us from our higher purposes in life and also from loving others and ourselves unconditionally. We are not here on earth to please people, we are here to evolve spiritually and pursue our true calling. By trying to pander to others all the time, we neglect our own evolution, diminish our self-esteem (which becomes dependent on how others perceive us) and usually wind up being heavily relied on by others. People will never learn to take responsibility for their actions if there is always someone there to do it for them. If we can take a step back, we can allow others to walk their own path in the way that is right for them and take charge of our own lives.

If we become angry, bitter and aggressive individuals as a consequence of our inability to reconcile with our past, then we are utilising our pent up guilt as a tool to bash people with. Unless we seek to address this issue, only one outcome will ensue, a miserable, malevolent existence for ourselves that is largely painted with deep self-destructive resentments and an unwillingness to face up to the reality of our lives. Again, this demonstrates a reluctance to learn from life's lessons and move onto to a better, healthier way of living. If we cannot learn, we cannot evolve. By hoarding our guilt we neglect to nourish our well-being and foster the expansion of both our Universal awareness and wisdom. To truly be healed, we must be able to come to terms with and then release the past.

The exercise below is called Recognising and Releasing Past Guilt and will allow you to accept responsibility for the mistakes you have made in life, renounce any responsibility that was not yours and then in time, move on. It is important to remember that many of the events in our lives have more than one culpable person.

When you think back to your past, try to see the events from a more objective point of view, as if you are an outsider looking in on your life. Watch what was happening around you, so that you can perceive where liability rests with you (if at all) and where it rests with others. For example, if you were abused, verbally or physically, as a young child, you were completely blame free at that time, because your parents were in a position of responsibility and no one has the right to treat a child in that manner. In this sort of situation, it is utterly futile trying to understand what you could possibly have done to provoke your parents, because you were just a child at the time and did not know any better.

However, if you then reach adulthood and start to become a bully, you cannot blame your childhood experiences and portray yourself as a victim. As an adult, you need to take responsibility for your behaviour. If you refuse to do this and always seek to place the blame with others you will forever be fighting a losing battle. However much we might not wish to acknowledge it, all of us have made mistakes in our lives and we should aim to make amends for our irresponsible actions. Playing the victim card or being resentful does us no favours.

This exercise will require you to make a list of all the events in your life that you feel guilty about and face up to those situations. I have to state that this may well be a painful experience for you. The most valuable opportunities for self-development in life are rarely easy. However, once you have fully accepted your responsibilities and let go of those that were not yours, you will feel like a huge ball and chain, that was dragging you down has been cast away from you.

Deal with one event from your life at a time. Do not try to solve everything at once. Healing the past is an incredibly time consuming process, it can take a whole lifetime or even longer. Furthermore, do not attempt to move on until you have accepted your accountability and relinquished the past. It is easy to say the right words but much harder to live by them. Neither the Universe, God or your soul is a fool and they will know if you are distorting the facts when you say you have accepted whatever blame was yours.

Over time, gradually work your way down the list of past situations until you have cleared them all away. If new things crop up that you had not thought of previously, add them to the list in the appropriate place and deal with them, as and when it is necessary. Take this exercise seriously, put real thought and effort into it and you will eventually reap the benefits of your altruism.

Fig 8.1

Fig 8.2

Exercises

Recognising and Releasing Past Guilt

1. Grab a piece of paper or two and a pen for this exercise. Think back through your entire life and write down all the things you can think of from your past that you feel guilty about.

2. When you have written your list, prioritise it in ascending order from the things you feel most guilty about, to the things you feel least guilty about.

3. Sit down comfortably either on the floor in seiza (on your knees with your bottom resting on your heels) or in agura (cross-legged) or on a chair. Make sure your back is straight. Place your palms in gassho (prayer position) in front of your chest.

4. Breathe in slowly through your nose, for a count of four. Hold your breath for four, then breathe out through your mouth for a count of four. Hold your breath for four and repeat the breathing process for several minutes or until you feel relaxed.

5. Rest your palms face down on your lap and take a deep breath, in through your nose and out through your mouth. Visualise the whole room filled with pure white Light and allow that Light to permeate your body.

6. Place your left hand on the top of your chest, in the middle and your right hand at the bottom of your chest, in the middle, so your hands run parallel (Fig 8.1).

7. Look at the past event at the top of your list that you feel most guilty about. Silently say to yourself, or out loud, with meaning and purpose, seven times, "I take responsibility for my actions at the time of .....(and read out the event you are feeling guilty about) for whatever responsibility is mine."

8. Look again at the past event at the top of your list. Silently say to yourself, or out loud, with meaning and purpose, seven times, "I let go of the responsibility at the time of.....(again read out the particular event) for whatever responsibility was not mine."

9. Place your palms over the sides of your forehead, completely covering your temples (Fig 8.2). Silently say to yourself, or out loud, with meaning and purpose, seven times, "I let go of this event, I accept the lessons I have learned from it. I grow in wisdom from letting it go. The Light of the Universe please allow me to move on, if it is within divine love and blessing."

10. Place your hands in gassho (prayer position) in front of your chest and bow to the Universe.

Chapter Nine

Self-Acceptance

Self-acceptance can only follow after a complete reconciliation with your past, so be sure to have fulfilled the criteria for that goal before moving onto this one.

We all long for self-acceptance and while some of us do it with relative ease, others find this to be the most testing challenge of their entire lives. Some people purposely refuse to accept themselves, often as a result of diminished self-esteem and consequently they perpetuate various life cycles of self-destructive and fruitless behaviour.

Accepting ourselves does not imply that we possess no desire to improve ourselves rather that we are not tied into a relentless ego battle, where we divide our being into separate segments. This is highly unproductive. If we are constantly fighting an inner battle, we delay our self-growth and spiritual progress, as well as giving ourselves a niggling headache, that just won't subside.

True self-acceptance can only be achieved through an intuitive connection. We need to be guided by our souls and rather than fitting into the moulds society has crafted for us, we need to aspire to the spiritual souls within us. We need to become divine, by embracing the divine within. As long as we pursue our physical and emotional desires at the expense of our spiritual well-being, we cannot truly accept ourselves. It is difficult to accept something inevitably flawed when residing within us is something so inimitably perfect. However, rather than punishing ourselves for what we have not yet become, we need to accept where we are now and make positive efforts to flourish spirituality.

It is essential for all of us to be able to look at our lives, understand where we are now, accept where we are now and then look ahead to where we need to be in the future. This will thus avoid any later recurrence of old past conflicts. A big part of self-acceptance is, learning from the past, accepting where we are in the present and using those life experiences to make healthy changes in the future.

Our past, as much as we may abhor it sometimes, is a part of who we are and if we determinedly choose to ignore its very existence, we are in a state of denial about our true selves. As I have mentioned numerous times, the experiences we go through in life act as invaluable lessons for us and if we ignore those past lessons, or behave as if they never occurred, we are in danger of going backwards instead of evolving. The past created our present, whether for 'bad' or 'good' and we need to accept what we have become and then we can endeavour to better ourselves in every way.

If you can accept yourself, you have made a giant leap in personal growth and will find it much easier to move onto the next level in your development.

Accepting yourself means coming to terms fully with **everything** about yourself, including all the things you don't necessarily relish facing up to and all the things you dislike about yourself. To effectively achieve this goal, you need to understand completely, within the core of your being that our physical existence is transient. Too many people are repelled by their physical appearance or obsessed with every physical aspect and detail of their bodies. Remember that your body is a temporary, yet still completely valuable, vessel to carry you through life. On the one hand you need to cherish your body and treat it with respect, on the other, you need to understand its impermanent nature and not get bogged down with your own physicality.

Treasure your body mentally and physically. Nourish your body with the right ingredients. Give your body regular exercise to keep it energised and strong. This advice really belongs in the Be Healthy section following this one, but it is also an important part of being able to accept yourself.

If you are completely neglecting your physical health, you will inherently be clinging onto an inner guilt and will not be able to facilitate a positive self-image. Accepting the body you were given is a pre-requisite to being a happier and freer individual, demolishing your body is not. If you establish a healthy body you can establish a healthy mindset. If we are reckless with our bodies, we are reckless with our souls. We need to nurture our bodies for our own health and spiritual development, not purely for appearance.

Of course, even if we are all the healthiest we can be many of us still have insecurities about our appearance. These are usually fostered by our culture, upbringing, environment and other people's attempts to lower our morale, to boosting their own lacklustre self-esteem. Once you are more connected with your true spiritual nature, you will place less value on the restrictions placed on you by your culture, environment and less conscious individuals, because you will have a higher awareness and appreciation of your Universal purpose. This connection brings forth your own previously dormant gifts and by understanding your true purpose your self-esteem will be elevated. I will discuss more about fostering a healthy body in the next section.

It is imperative to accept the choices you have made in life, however wrong you may feel they have been. Our choices form priceless lessons that burgeon our spiritual growth if we choose to learn. If we indeed want to grow as human beings, we **must** learn from them. Refusing to learn will wedge us into a cycle of continuous negative patterns of behaviour. If you can learn, you can come to accept yourself, because you will see the value of the choices you have made relative to where you are in the present and where you will be in the future. Needlessly punishing yourself for all your mistakes in life, will only make you utterly miserable and unable to see the value in anything life throws at you.

As the adage goes, appreciate yourself, because if you don't no one else will. If you fail to do this you will end up abusing your body, mind and soul and then other people will abuse you as well, because you have made it so easy for them. When you portray a particular persona, people react to that portrayal and will treat you in a certain way as a result. If you lie all the time, people will see you as a liar, mistrust you and measure the information they proffer to you. If you always give people the benefit of the doubt, whether they deserve it or not, people will start to take advantage of your good nature. If you are promiscuous, people will see you in terms of your body, as an object, rather than as a human being.

Potentially, if you pursue a facade for long enough, you can become so far removed from your true higher self that your ethics are values are distorted or disbanded. If you ever get to the stage where you have lost your intuitive ethics, you will not know the difference between right and wrong.

You know how hard it can be yourself, as an outsider, when you see people that you love harming themselves. Try to look at your life more objectively and see the affects of your self-destructive attitudes and actions on those around you. There is enough pain and suffering in the world, don't make your own. Remember, consistently being hard on yourself will only cause you grief and much unhappiness during and after this life. Cut yourself some slack, learn every second of your life, love everyday that you are alive and accept who you are. If you can achieve this, you are well on the road to inner peace and tranquillity.

The exercise below is entitled Accepting Yourself and will aid you in appreciating where you are in life and how you can move on positively from this.

The breathing technique used, will help you to expel negative emotional traumas from your navel and chest areas. Many people store their pain in these locations of the body, so by pushing this pain out of your body you can start to adopt a clearer perspective on your life and self-image.

The visualisation utilised in this exercise, of yourself in the past and present immersed in white Light, will facilitate a healing process within your emotional body. This will allow you to eventually let go of negative ingrained attitudes that you may have possessed for your entire life. As you visualise your past selves merging into you, as you are now, you will discover a newfound acceptance for yourself that will cultivate a healthier, more positive and more spiritually aware state of mind. As ever, practise makes perfect. You need to put the effort in, to see results.

Exercise

Accepting Yourself

1. Sit down comfortably on the floor in seiza (on your knees with your bottom resting on your heels) or in agura (cross-legged) or on a chair. Make sure your back is straight. Place your hands in gassho (prayer position) in front of your chest.

2. Breathe in through your nose, slowly and deeply and breathe out through your mouth, making a whispering *Hoo* sound as you breathe out. Do this for between three and five minutes.

3. Silently say to yourself, or out loud, with meaning and purpose, seven times, "I accept myself for everything I have done, I am constantly learning, I have moved on."

4. Visualise a spiral of white Light coming down through space as far up as the eye can see. Allow the Light to enter the crown of your head and continue spiralling through your entire body. See the spirals gradually become thicker, until you eventually have a solid wall of Light, coming down from above and filling your entire body.

5. Within the Light, inside of your body, picture vividly a mini-version of yourself, as you were at the age of three. Allow the Light in your body to be absorbed into your past self.

6. Repeat three times the affirmation from step 3.

7. Within the Light inside of your body, aside the three-year old version of yourself, visualise another mini-version of yourself, as you were at the age of fifteen. Again allow the bright Light within your body to be absorbed into your past self.

8. Repeat three times the affirmation from step 3.

9. Within the Light inside of your body, between the three and fifteen-year old mini-versions of yourself, visualise another mini-version of yourself, as you are now. Again, allow the bright Light within your body to be absorbed into the current version of yourself.

10. Repeat three times the affirmation from step 3.

11. Visualise the three versions of you standing side by side, filled with beautiful Light. Picture the three and the fifteen-year old versions of yourself, that are on either side of you merging into the current version of you, so you are left with you as you are now.

12. Visualise the Light within the current version of you, becoming brighter and brighter, until eventually the image merges into the pure white Light inside you. So, in effect all you can see now is the wall of Light from space filling your body again.

13. Silently say to yourself or out loud, with meaning and purpose, seven times, "The past and me are one and the same, I learned from the past, I accept who I became. I accept myself as I am that I may grow by the Light."

14. At the end, bow to the Universe in gassho (prayer position) with your hands in front of your chest.

Chapter Ten

Expressing Your True Self

One of the most demanding challenges I have faced in life is learning to express myself freely. Coming from a place of fear as a young child, I spent much of my life desperately trying to please those around me. Chameleon like, I would distort my personality to suit whomever happened to be in my company. I had a new face for every situation. My anger, sadness, stress, worries and the host of other emotions that beleaguered my being were carefully buried under a face of congeniality. This, inevitably resulted in me being a sturdy shoulder to lean on, yet simultaneously I became very reckless as I fought my true nature and hid under a blanket of 'I'm OKs.' This flagrant denial of my true emotions forced me ever further away from my spiritual nature, until I became so detached that I lost my sense of right and wrong, to quite a degree.

Every day, atrocities take place all over the world, emblazoned upon the television screens and printed press. Do you ever pause to wonder how someone can thoughtlessly stab someone without any hint of remorse or empathy? I can give some slight insight into this. The perpetrator has lost all connection to their true spiritual nature. They are so far away from their true self that they really have no sense of morality or justice. Inflicting pain on others, for them is mere child's play for they are in such a dark, cold lonely place that they cannot see the Light. Fear means nothing to them, not because they have faith, but because they crave more power and will do anything they can to fulfil their most sinister desires. Some of them can crawl out of the vicious spell they are under, by being shown the truth. Others will always remain in their cold dark place, because they do not believe in the truth.

If we have no soul connection, we effectively have no intuition, until we restore it through personal development. If we are disconnected from our spiritual nature, we lose our sense of unconditional love and compassion, instead turning to the fulfilment of our basest physical desires. By doing this we express our physical and not spiritual selves, which is the antithesis of enlightenment.

Repressing your emotions is a recipe for disaster that can lead, not only to negative patterns of behaviour, but also to a severely damaged body. I wholeheartedly believe that our emotional traumas create negative energies within our aura (a bio-magnetic field that runs four metres around our body). As the years go by and we continually develop more traumas and stifle our true feelings, the negative energies become denser and get drawn closer and closer to the body. Eventually, if the issues have not been addressed, it is my personal belief that the energies can enter our bodies and create a physical illness of some kind, whether its cancer, a stomach disorder or some other health related problem. Stored emotional traumas can affect us so severely that the damage done is irreversible.

I cannot stress enough, how important it is to express your emotions, rather than burying your feelings and letting them eat away at you slowly. Do not be afraid to let people see your real self. It may be a shock to those around you initially, because for so long they have become accustomed to seeing you as someone different. However, once they acclimatise to the real you, they will hopefully appreciate you all the more for it and you too will be infinitely happier. If they do not like the real you, tough! They will either have to learn to deal with it or get on with bettering their own lives instead of musing over yours.

Sometimes, even the people close to us are envious of our progress, because it makes more apparent to them, the deficiencies in their own character. Try to raise them up to your level rather than sinking down to theirs. If they do not want to be helped in any way, then let them be. They may come to regret it later on. Ultimately it's not your problem to deal with. Your aim should be to follow your higher path in life.

This may all seem somewhat cruel, but most of us have to learn lessons the hard way in life and by doing this we value them all the more. You will demand far greater respect from others, if you are not an easy target for people to aim their frustrations at. If we are too passive, allowing people mould us; they can tend to perceive us, either on a conscious or subconscious level, as vulnerable prey to have a pick at when they are feeling inadequate about themselves.

There is no common sense whatsoever in allowing yourself to be moulded out of all recognition. Power seekers love nothing more than the thrill of hounding the weak, to feed their escalating egos. If you are blatantly, honestly and forthrightly being your true self in the face of all situations, those sorts of people will not be able to steal your precious energy and weaken your self-esteem. Your courage, awareness and insight will stand you in good stead and no matter what anyone does to you; they will not be able to beat down the truly spiritual being that you have become.

I understand completely that expressing yourself can be an extremely daunting and even painful task. If you have held all your pain within you for your entire life and people have come to see you in a certain way, suddenly releasing all that pain and speaking out can seem overwhelmingly scary and even a little bit selfish. People who repress their emotions often do it for fear of hurting the feelings of those around them and for fear of reprisal. I can assure you that 99% of the time, they will not be nearly as upset as you imagine they will be and if they are, they will soon get over it. Of course, you should always approach the subject matter with tact and diplomacy, but endeavour to be honest.

We often rerun possible outcomes over and over again in our heads, every time imagining an even worse conclusion. We are terribly frightened that the other person involved in the interaction will judge us harshly and come to dislike our nature. The important thing to remember is that people are very resilient and in many cases, they care far less about our reactions than we think they do.

Most of us have been involved in situations where we have blown a gasket at someone, because they kept pushing and pushing at us until we could take no more. They may have got a bit upset, a bit shocked or even been furious but they got over it. I doubt that the one event where you spoke your mind frankly, dominated their entire life. Being hurtful for the sake of causing pain is a different issue, but expressing yourself, rather than bottling up emotions is essential to your happiness. In saying that though, it is far better in the long run to always speak out your thoughts and emotions as they arise, rather than letting them accumulate into an erupting volcano of fury. You will save yourself and those around you, from a lot of grief. Express yourself with diplomacy.

When you have overcome the fear of expressing your true self once, it will be much easier to set the ball rolling and do it over and over again. Perhaps, plan beforehand what you would like to say to someone, so you don't have to fumble for the right words when you do talk to them. If you want to be taken seriously, state your words with conviction. Be strong and resilient in your demeanour and have faith in your own integrity and intuition. Let the other person know that you are not to be toyed with and you most certainly are going to stand your ground. It is an extremely difficult thing to do, but the fear will almost certainly be much worse than the upshot, so be brave and bold and express your true self.

The exercise below, entitled Self-Expression, will begin to accustom you to staring intently at yourself in the mirror and seeing beyond your physical body, to the beauty of your inner self. By seeing into the Light of your soul, you will be able to embrace and speak the truth of your true higher self to others. This technique forms a connection between accepting your true self and expressing your true self. You are seeing and saying as you are, without pretence or fake mannerisms adopted to help you blend you into your environment.

The concentration on the throat region is used near the end of the exercise, because people who repress their emotions can have a tendency to store negative energy and pain in this area. The hands cupping the throat will allow the affirmation used to be embedded into your throat and release the negative energy over a period of time.

Remember, that self-expression is not a very easy goal to undertake, so this exercise will need to be practised at least once a day and it will require a conscious commitment from you as well, to speak your mind more frequently. Set yourself realistic targets for how long it will take you to attain this state of mind.

Exercise

Self-Expression

1. Stand or sit in front of a mirror (wherever you have one in your house). If you are sitting, then sit in seiza (on your knees with your bottom resting on your heels) or in agura (cross-legged) or on a chair. Place your hands in gassho (prayer) position in front of your chest.

2. Focus very intently on yourself in the mirror. Notice all the little details of your physical body. Don't pass judgement on what you see (no ruminating over the size of your bum or the big zit on your chin!) just concentrate on it. Look at yourself, as if you were examining some amazing precious jewel.

3. Either turn away from the mirror completely, or close your eyes and visualise a white Light, so bright it is almost impossible to look at, coming down through space as far up as the eye can see. See the Light enter the crown of your head from above, like a radiant beam and allow the Light to enter your entire body from your head through to the tips of your toes.

4. Visualise the Light spreading and engulfing the entire room. Breathe very slowly and deeply, continuing this visualisation for several minutes.

5. Turn to face the mirror again, or open your eyes and slightly de-focusing your eyes, look at yourself in the mirror again. Rather than looking at your physical body, look inside your body to your higher self. Look into your

eyes to the eye of your soul. See bright Light shining from within you.

6. Allow the Light inside of you, to grow brighter and brighter, so that your physical body is engulfed in beautiful white Light.

7. Look into your eyes in the mirror and silently say, to yourself or out loud seventeen times with meaning and purpose, "I see the real me and I am able to speak the words I need to express."

8. Re-focus your gaze back to normal and again stare intently at your physical self, noticing every detail. Cup your hands around your throat. Look at your physical self in the mirror and silently say to yourself, or out loud, seventeen times, with meaning and purpose, "I see the real me and I am able to speak the words I need to express."

9. Place your hands in gassho (prayer position) in front of your chest. Take a deep breath in and out through your nose and smile at yourself in the mirror.

10. When you have finished, bow to the Universe.

Chapter Eleven

Healthy Living

To be enlightened and fully self-healed we need to be living healthily. Our bodies require very pure and simple foods that nourish our organs and thus it follows, nurture our souls. We need to be truly conscious of how we live our lives in every way and an enlightened soul would naturally understand the implications of a poorly tended body. Someone who is highly spiritually developed, by virtue of their purity of thought, would not physically be able to tolerate substances that were damaging to the body. I will explain this in more detail.

I believe that our bodies, like everything else in this Universe, are made up of energy. Our minds and spirits are also made up of higher frequency energy. If we lead very physical, desire driven lifestyles our bodies vibrate at low-level frequencies. This is because being concerned only with mortal, non-spiritual matters we are steered away from the much higher and lighter frequencies of our Divine spiritual bodies.

When we become more spiritually elevated, (closer to our spiritual bodies or souls), we begin to vibrate at higher electromagnetic frequencies, as our thoughts and our actions become purer and far less self-indulgent. As this occurs, our bodies become increasingly cleansed and 'lighter.' Due to our increased spiritual awareness and connection with our higher selves, our bodies wish fervently to stay that way. Thus at this stage, if we attempt to smoke a cigarette for instance, we may find that it makes us incredibly nauseous, even potentially causing us to vomit. This is our bodies' way of signalling to us that they are not happy with the substance we have provided. They may respond in less harsh or harsher ways, but when we become more aware, it limits what we are able to do in certain respects. Our bodies begin to reject anything that is harmful to them. This could include environmental toxins such as car fumes and cigarette smoke or unhealthy foods. If we choose to persistently eat damaging foods, our frequency can drop and we could potentially develop health issues and compromise our spiritual development.

It really is essential, as a spiritual and as a developed human being, to take good care of your body, to cherish that body and treat it with respect. You cannot sincerely have love for yourself and heal, if you are poisoning your body on a daily basis. Poor diet costs the National Health Service in the UK billions of pounds per year.

We would all do well to pay very close attention to our eating habits. This doesn't mean you should suddenly embark on a lifelong guilt trip about your diet. Just be aware of what you are consuming and what sort of environments you place yourself in. Try to consciously think if this is the right thing you should be doing, for the fruitful progress of your body, mind and soul.

Start making positive changes in your life now. As an example, if you normally consume three chocolate bars a day, perhaps cut down to two or three a week and make them organic chocolate bars. This way, you will know that you are consuming a far healthier option.

If you usually go out to a pub or club twice a week, try and cut it down initially to three times a month and only have a couple of alcoholic beverages, instead of getting intoxicated. On the other times when you would typically be out drinking, perhaps try a different, more holistic activity such as visiting an alternative therapist, heading to a spa for the weekend or having a healthy themed night in with your friends. These are just starting blocks of course, but as time goes on you will discover a much healthier, happier you, who gleans pleasure from the small yet much more important things in life. Just the knowledge that you are fostering your own well-being, will give you a wonderful sense of inner contentment.

A spiritually advanced individual can be completely content, sitting in a room alone, without any distractions, just contemplating. If you cannot do this, you need to ask yourself why. The answer is very often a fear of the unknown or buried emotional traumas. People often clamour for things to do to avoid being alone. If you sit alone in a room for long enough, you will realise that you are never alone. This is an exercise worth undertaking.

As you grow spiritually, you will find that your food preferences naturally alter anyway. An elevated mind and spirit would not wish to, or feel the need to, indulge in the unhealthy option on any level, because that would defy the very logic of being aware.

If you were an ardent vegetable hater previously, you may find that after raising your spiritual awareness you will suddenly start to crave vegetables. Indeed, you may laugh at this notion, but it does happen. I used to drink caffeine every single day, once upon a time. I thought I would never give it up. My indulgence stretched amongst other things, to scoffing chocolate and cakes every day and gobbling plenty of meat and fish.

A couple of months or so after undertaking my Reiki course, I felt guided by God and my intuition, to become a Vegan. I did this instantly and gave up caffeine completely, henceforth. I never once missed my caffeine fix or eating meat products, because I so loved my healthy, nourishing new food habits.

My unconditional love for all living things extended to such an extent that I could not justify eating animal products to myself, because I knew that my body didn't need them to be healthy and I could not bare the thought of the animals suffering. Occasionally, I would eat vegan organic chocolate bars but I found I could no longer tolerate them anymore and my cravings had ceased anyway, so I abandoned all sugary foods. Besides, a poor diet in the past had caused me to have health issues that needed to be resolved by eating healthily and nourishing my body. There is nothing like the shock of an illness to make you realise how damaging your lifestyle has been.

This was all a very natural process for me. It wasn't difficult or forced and was absolutely nothing like going on a troublesome diet, where you desperately crave all the foods you shouldn't be eating. I simply did not want, on any level, to eat anything that wasn't healthy anymore. People would try to coax me into eating biscuits and cakes, but to no avail because I had no desire for them and anyhow, I knew all about the incredibly harmful ingredients such as hydrogenated fats and artificial sweeteners that lurked within. When I look at a cake now I do not see a delicious, tasty treat, but a potential cardiac arrest!

I am by no means suggesting that everyone has to become vegan or abandon all treats; this was my path in life and the right thing for me to do for my higher self. I beseech you all to listen to your own higher selves and do what is right for you, walk your own higher path because you can never walk anyone else's and you will inevitably become incredibly lost if you attempt to.

If you are not sure how to maintain a healthy body, then do plenty of research, consult your doctor and perhaps, if necessary, a nutritional expert. Just think pure and simple ingredients and you will be at a fantastic starting place. You cannot go wrong with plenty of fresh fruit and vegetables, jam packed full of antioxidants (preferably organically grown as these are not cultivated in nutrient deficient artificial fertilisers and then sprayed with pesticides, herbicides, fungicides and other nasties).

Beans, tofu and lentils, consumed in the appropriate quantities, are incredibly healthy alternatives to meat and fish for protein, if you are vegan or vegetarian.

Try to avoid packaged, processed and convenience foods, which usually contain additives, colourings, flavour enhancers, hydrogenated fats, high quantities of salt and sugar and generally, lack nutritional value.

Caffeine is a temporary stimulant at best, so be very careful of consuming high levels of products containing this ingredient. Try to substitute with de-caffeinated green tea, yerba mate or other herbal teas such as: chamomile, liquorice, dandelion, rosehip, nettle and peppermint.

Rather than imbibing high volumes of fizzy drinks for a quick energy fix, perhaps invest in a juicer and create some delicious fruit and vegetable juices. If you have never drunk a fresh home made fruit or vegetable juice before, you will be amazed at how energised it will make you feel. You can sense that your cells are receiving intense nourishment, as soon as you take a sip.

We are always hearing in the press and on television about Essential Fatty Acids (EFAs), or the 'good' fats that perform vital functions within the body such as: maintaining cell membranes and normalising cholesterol levels. To ensure you get enough EFAs, it is necessary to eat plenty of, seeds, vegetables, grains and nuts. EFAs can also be found in oils such as: sunflower, sesame, wheat germ, flaxseed, pumpkin, fish, rapeseed, hemp and walnut oils and in spirulina, a wild blue-green algae.

Get plenty of fibre in your diet, which helps your body to eliminate waste products, amongst other crucial functions.

If you are a meat fanatic, conceivably you could cut down the quantity of meat you eat each week, eating other protein sources as well, such as soya products, tahini, beans and lentils. It is worth noting, that organic meat is gleaned from animals that have generally speaking, been reared in a much healthier environment and it tends to be of a superior standard, with lower levels of dangerous fats and antibiotic substances.

If you are planning on undergoing a completely new dietary regime visit a qualified nutritionist registered with The British Association for Nutritional Therapy (BANT), or the relevant governing body in your country and always consult your doctor if you have any queries about health issues, or intend to embark upon a new health plan.

If you are not used to eating healthily, it might initially be a bit of a challenge for you and you may suffer withdrawal effects from ingredients such as caffeine and sugar, but after a short time the benefits you reap will be so great that you will never want to return to unhealthy eating or living again. In fact, your body will most likely not allow that to happen, it will rapidly make you aware if you have consumed something it does not approve of.

If you treat your body with reverence, it will serve you well and you will be more likely to value yourself highly and develop strong self-esteem and self-worth. As I mentioned previously, you cannot love yourself if you are neglecting any one part of your being. Your body is infinitely precious and should be treated as such. Comfort eating or other poor dietary habits are a sign that there is some emotional unrest within you that needs to be addressed. So, in essence you cannot be completely healed without a healthy, happy body.

The exercise below is entitled Healthy Living and will aid you in raising your own awareness about nurturing and nourishing your body. This technique will enable you to perceive the consequences of an unhealthy lifestyle, through a meditation that will help to cleanse your inner organs to foster enhanced well-being. You will place the affirmations used into various regions of your body, mind and soul to ensure that you really are able to consciously and subconsciously improve your health.

By allowing your spiritual body to float up into the Light, you will be expanding both your Universal and self-awareness and encouraging deep healing to take place on all levels. The greater the self-healing you achieve, on all levels, the more spiritually advanced you become and the more likely you will be to adopt positive, healthy attitudes and live in the way that is right for you.

If you continue this exercise diligently, with a serious state of mind and for a long enough period of time, you will be incredibly guided about where you should be directing your attention in relation to your physical condition.

By rooting your head in the Light above and your feet on the ground, in this exercise you will be able to foster inner wisdom, courage and an ability to always have foresight and clarity of vision that will guide you correctly through life.

Try to practise this exercise at least three times a week, more if you have the time available. Remember, don't be harsh on yourself and adapt at a pace that is right for you. Accept change when change comes and everything will fall into place.

Don't force yourself to change your life. If you have to force yourself, then you are not in the right place yet to be making the changes. This is your path and you need to take it at a pace that is right for you and you only. Do no compare your path to the paths of others, just focus on where you are right now and where you are heading. Trust in what you know. Be accepting of what the Universe sends your way, without constantly pre-empting what will be in store for you on your higher path.

Fig 11.1

Fig 11.2

Exercise

Healthy Living

1. Sit down comfortably on the floor in seiza (on your knees with your bottom resting on your heels) or in agura (cross-legged) or on a chair. Make sure your back is straight. Place your hands in gassho (prayer position) in front of your chest.

2. Breathe in slowly through your nose for a count of four. Hold your breath for four, then breathe out through your mouth for a count of four. Repeat this breathing process for several minutes or until you feel relaxed.

3. Visualise that inside the centre of your forehead, chest and navel areas are three glowing balls of white Light, becoming brighter and brighter. Sit for a couple of minutes remaining focused on these globes of Light.

4. Silently say to yourself, or out loud, with meaning and purpose, seven times, "Allow me to see the price of doing what damages me, so that I may truly be healthy."

5. Visualise the balls of Light expanding through your body, so eventually your entire body is glowing with white Light.

6. Place your palms over your eyes (Fig 11.1) and repeat the affirmation from step 4, seven times.

7. Place your palms over your navel (Fig 11.2) and repeat the affirmation from step 4, seven times.

8. Place your hands in gassho (prayer position) in front of your chest.

9. Visualise your spiritual body absorbed in white Light, floating off the ground. See your body lifting higher. Allow yourself to float through the roof and into the sky, amongst the clouds and the birds. Continue lifting up into outer space surrounded by stars, planets and galaxies, until you reach a beautiful bright white Light. Allow yourself to enter this white Light and become one with the Light. Feel warmth, love and serenity wash over your entire being.

10. Silently say to yourself, or out loud, seven times, "The Light of the Universe, allow me to see how I must live to truly be healthy."

11. Continue to float higher up into the Light. Remain here for between five and twenty minutes.

12. Repeat the affirmation from step 10, seven times.

13. Float up higher until you have reached as far as you can go.

14. Repeat the affirmation from step 10, seven times.

15. Visualise your spiritual body filled with the affirmation. Gently, allow the lower half of your body to stretch back down to earth, with your head still in the Light. See your lower body stretching down, with your legs and feet descending through space, the sky and the roof and back onto the ground, where you are seated.

16. Maintain this visualisation for a few moments and then when you have finished, bow to the Universe.

Part Four

Being Truth, Living Truth

Introduction to Part Four

"The truth exists for all who will see the truth and all who will let living the truth become their tenet for life. Always let honesty be your guide, open your ears and open your eyes for the truth is elusive to the many"

By the time you embark upon your journey of being and living the truth, you should already have stared reality boldly in the face and understood both its infinite glory and immeasurable torment. We can flee from the truth for a while, perhaps, for some, for a whole lifetime or numerous lifetimes, but we cannot avoid it ad infinitum.

The truth is at the core of omniscient, omnipresent, omnipotent Light for whom we dwell on earth. If we do not want to hear and see reality now, we will be forced to see it in due course and our failure to do so previously, will severely affect out spiritual path. If you do nothing else in life, seek reconciliation with your intuitive higher self. If you choose to set your intuition free and listen intently, you will find and become the truth eventually.

Aim to know yourself completely. You have all the answers you could ever need, if you just endeavour to listen to your own inner voice. It may begin as a whisper, but with perseverance and right living, it will grow to a scream. When that happens and when you comply with the guidance of your highest spiritual nature, you will come to know and to **be** the embodiment of the eternal Light, the truth that is hidden from the many.

You should now be at the stage, from your work in the previous chapters, where you have: established a connection with your true higher self, confronted the reality of the world surrounding you, significantly self-healed and lived a healthy lifestyle that is conducive to your spiritual evolution and self-development. This section will aid you in fostering a much more heightened awareness, such that you will be pure of body, mind and spirit, and you should be leaping towards the realisation of enlightenment. This is of course, if you maintain your state of being and do not perform any action that would compromise your spiritual connection.

In Chapter Twelve, you will learn how to maintain a happy balance in your life. The term balance is often widely misinterpreted and used as justification, by some individuals, to indulge in activities that they know are detrimental to their well-being. This would, of course, be a denial of the truth, so not something, at this point in your spiritual development that you should be doing for your productive self-growth.

In reality, balance, from a spiritual perspective implies that you are grounded in the work you are fulfilling on earth. If you are so caught up in your spiritual body that you retreat into your spiritual self, you will be distancing yourself from the earthbound activities you are required to tend to for your spiritual purpose. Conversely, many people seek refuge in their physical existence and neglect their spiritual nature. This too creates an imbalance, though this is more detrimental than the former. To balance the scales you need to be able to carry your true higher self with you in every part of your life. Your environment should not cause you to stifle your real spiritual nature, but rather you should seek to raise others up to their own true spiritual self, or else let them be if they are not apt or willing to do so at that point in time.

Chapter Thirteen will help you to raise your spiritual and Universal awareness, allowing you to witness yet more personal and Universal truths. By continually elevating your spiritual awareness, you will be given more and more insights into your own journey and into the journey of those around you, the earth, the Universe and far beyond. When you reach enlightenment you will know all there is to know and will have no more spiritual questions to ask.

Following this, you will discover how you can begin to love everyone and everything unconditionally and realise the implications of this. It has absolutely nothing to do with fake appreciation or mock niceties. Part of loving unconditionally is allowing people to learn their own lessons in life, even if you know they should be behaving differently. The technique used in this section will aid you in standing back from situations and becoming more healthily detached from people.

Once you are able to love everyone and everything unconditionally, you can work on fully accepting your higher purpose on earth. There needs to be unconditional acceptance of our higher paths regardless of the circumstances we find ourselves in. We need to trust in our intuition and in God (if you believe in God).

Finally, once all of these goals have been successfully attained you can work towards entirely being and living the truth. You will carry your spiritual self with you wherever you go and never try to hide from your true spiritual nature. When your peers, family and work colleagues see the real you, they may be utterly astonished by your transformation. Some of the responses of those around you will be incredibly positive and uplifting, whilst others will be negative and unwarrantably critical. This should not faze you, for you will be guided by your highest power, your spiritual self and not a soul on this earth or beyond should be able to cripple your growth. Your courage, determination and true strength of connection should carry you victoriously through this life and beyond. The Light will shine forth from your eyes because you have become and you are living the truth. When you achieve this state of being, be immensely proud of yourself and abundant in humility. We can only reach enlightenment if we are humble in the face of the Universe.

Chapter Twelve

Being Balanced

Balance, from the perspective of our journey on earth, refers to our ability to maintain steadfast in fulfilling our true purpose for being here, all the time retaining our spirituality in our day to day living and constant interactions with those around us. We need to have our feet very firmly planted on the ground and our head reaching to the 'heavens' for wisdom. Our body, mind and soul must be in a state of equilibrium, not controlled purely by our physical desires or lead by irrational emotions.

In Part One, I spoke of our holy trinity of bodies that can become detached, due to our lifestyles and interactions. Visualise these three bodies (physical, emotional and spiritual) as three circles. When we are solely driven by our corporeal selves, these circles of the physical, emotional and spiritual drift apart from one another, shooting off in all different directions, unable to communicate effectively with the other bodies. As we become more connected and balanced, these circles start to overlap and we can readily converse with our spiritual bodies or our intuition. Our goal is to bring these circles together so that there is one perfect circle, with no separation between the three bodies. This is enlightenment or 'oneness,' which I will explain in more detail in a later chapter.

If we become unbalanced, one or two of our bodies start to dominate over the others. If our physical body controls us, we associate happiness with realising our worldly desires and achieving everything we want, whether it is something we actually need, or otherwise. Our emotions become terribly confused and if we crave power, they become completely lost or suppressed under a blanket of pure adulterated ego. We go through life on a hunt for larger doses of authority, thriving on the weaknesses of others. Alternatively, we just search for happiness in all the wrong places, hoping that money and cheap thrills can buy us contentment.

With our emotional body taking charge, we can end up using our most irrational emotions to control others. Rather than bargaining with money or our bodies, we use our anger or tears to manipulate others. We cannot separate our true direction and needs in life, from the emotional crutches that we long for. Depression can prevail within us, confusing our emotions even more, making us entirely lost for all direction and purpose. We sink into the depths of our most wretched emotions, letting the traumas of our past breed anger and desolate loneliness, in a world we are confused by and with an inner self we cannot fathom. Our emotions are erupting all over the place and we cannot begin to reconcile ourselves with our physical, emotional or spiritual bodies, because all we know is that we long so dreadfully, for all our anguish and pain to be soothed away.

Our physical and emotional bodies may collaborate, creating a longing for worldly wealth and a buttress for our emotions. We sit and wistfully pine for a better abode, more products and a perfect partner who will love us so dearly that they will make up for our own lack of self-love. Or, we feign the search for our spirit, only wishing to hear what pleases our ears. With our plea for contentment we look to 'gurus' and false promise makers for easy options. We know in our heart of hearts that life's best lessons are the hardest learned but still, in vain, we blindly hunt for a quick fix to our life long troubles and bitterly entrenched inner turmoil.

Out of all the options, it is highly preferable to have your spiritual body leading the way, but if our heads are too far up in the clouds and our bodies are drifting further away from the earth, we are neglecting our earthly duties. We all come to earth to work, in one way or another, so we cannot neglect our higher paths indefinitely without consequences. If our journey is destined to involve us interacting with lots of people and we lock ourselves away from the world to ride high in the heavens, we are forgetting that we have extremely important tasks to perform. We will be given the chance to reside in the Light, once our work on earth is completed.

In reality, it is only for a short time that we inhabit the earth, so we should all aim to achieve as much as we possibly can spiritually, whilst we have the gift of living. By doing this, we can come to discover the real Life that awaits us after this one.

Try to bear in mind, that everyone on this planet has a distinct purpose and avoid making comparisons with others. There is absolutely no competition in spiritual development. Each soul that enters the earthly realm has a different journey to undertake and there is no hierarchy of a worldly nature on a Universal scale. Everyone's path in life is equally valid.

Maintaining elemental balance in our lives is vital for our personal growth and spiritual development. Any kind of imbalance could possibly result in some of the occurrences I have previously described to you. I believe that the negativity that pervades much of society is, for the most part, due to disconnected and imbalanced human beings wandering the planet looking for answers in all the wrong places, dominated by ego or a profound lack of direction in life. Balance is an absolute necessity to achieve any level of freedom and genuine happiness.

The exercise below is entitled Balancing Act and will allow you to clear negative energy from your body, helping you to more readily assess where the imbalances reside within you. It will also aid your understanding of what real balance within us naturally implies.

The beam of Light used in this technique will foster a harmonious balance between your mind, body and soul. Your head, heart and tanden are the bodily representations of the trinity of bodies that reside within us. The tanden represents the physical body, the heart the emotional body and the head the spiritual body. You will create an unbreakable connection that should ensure, with dedicated practise, that no individual or any external situation, can re-install an imbalance within you. By doing this you are developing your divine connection and fostering a profound understanding of yourself and the Universe. Practise this exercise at least three times a week.

Exercise

Balancing Act

1. Sit down comfortably either on the floor in seiza (on your knees with your bottom resting on your heels) or in agura (cross-legged) or on a chair. Make sure your back is straight. Place your hands in gassho (prayer position) in front of your chest.

2. Breathe in through your nose, slowly and deeply and breathe out through your mouth, making a whispering *Haa* sound as you breathe out. Feel the sound emanating from your stomach and inner organs. Do this for between three and five minutes.

3. Visualise a thin beam of white Light coming from above you as far up as the eye can see, entering your crown then passing through to your heart and your tanden (3cm below the navel).

4. Visualise this beam of Light as a connector, passing back and forth from your head, to your heart, to your tanden and back again. Each time you do this, feel the connection growing stronger.

5. As you maintain this visualisation, silently say to yourself, or out loud, with meaning and purpose, seven times, "I balance my body, mind and soul so that I may become one."

6. Repeat step 2 for a couple of minutes, whilst maintaining the visualisation of the connecting Light beam.

7. Still visualising the Light beam, silently say to yourself, or out loud, with meaning and purpose, seven times, "I have created a connection which no human can break, I will maintain this connection for my higher self's sake."

8. When you have finished, bow to the Universe.

Chapter Thirteen

Being Aware

Developing a true sense of balance in our lives will ensure that our insight, awareness and understanding, of the Universe and ourselves, has the potential for huge growth. Being aware is partially to do with having a profound comprehension of living a life conducive to spiritual progression. We cannot be spiritually aware if we are oblivious to or deny the reality of our lives and the Universe. Quite simply, ignorance prevents awareness. Beyond this, true awareness requires much more.

There are people in all walks of life that unwittingly live spiritual lifestyles, because they have always attempted to innately do what is right for their higher selves and spiritual paths (whether they believe in those paths or not). They are indeed spiritual, but this does not automatically make them **highly** aware on a divine level. This is because the awareness I speak of presumes a strong grasp of the very nature of the Universe and our place in the Universe. Awareness means knowing all that we need to know.

This is not something that comes easily to everyone. It is developed with much hard work and daily right, conscious living. Our divine awareness cannot thrive merely because we command it to, or wish that it would. It blossoms at a time when we are spiritually advanced enough to fully perceive what we have been shown. There is no point being shown the Light, if we can only see the dark.

Awareness comes to those who truly have knowledge and intuitive insight, because they are thoroughly ready to have their consciousness expanded and they are in a place where it will make sense to them. As awareness increases, it breeds further knowledge and we can come to know a great many things that remain hidden from most individuals. This knowledge is not a secret code that is unattainable, or reserved for a few people as such, rather many people make choices that steer them aware from Universal wisdom. The answers are there for anyone who is prepared to work for them.

When we do develop a higher awareness, it may be so intensely insightful that we yearn to head for the hilltops to scream it to all and sundry. Yet, this wisdom must be shared discerningly and only with those who are in the right place to understand, as we too have understood. It is futile trying to pass this acquired awareness onto someone who is in a wildly divergent state of being. For instance, if an individual has experienced a very heartbreaking bereavement they will likely be relatively inconsolable for a period of time, because they are traumatised by their loss. The bereaved can get lost in their memories and it can take years to recover from such a deep emotional trauma. This is completely understandable.

During the grieving process, someone incredibly well meaning may come along and say to the grief stricken person, "you know I had a near death experience once and it was the most wonderful experience ever. I never used to believe in life after death, but that experience showed me that we live on. I got to meet all my family and friends who had passed away and I was engulfed in the most exquisite Light that took away all my pain and sadness. I am sure that your friend, who has passed away, is now in that amazing, happy place. Do not feel sad for them because they have finally found peace."

These words may just wash over the bereaved person with no real impact. They may even make them feel very angry or confused, because at that moment in time they are feeling the sadness of their loss. They are so enveloped in anguish that they cannot see beyond the end of the deceased person's life on earth, either because they do not want to, or simply cannot. In time, they may come to believe that there is more to come after this life on earth, but at the time of their grief and bereavement they are in shock, too dumbstruck by the unfolding of events that have taken place and by their own emotional destituteness.

In this example, the well-wisher may have a raised level of awareness based on his or her own relevant personal experiences in life. However, the bereaved individual is not in a place spiritually or otherwise, to entirely comprehend the significance of the well-wisher's words. Their own level of awareness is completely different and they are at completely different stages in their lives. The bereaved person may one day believe what they were told, or they may never believe it. We cannot will someone to have Divine awareness, anymore than we can make ourselves possess awareness just because we desire it to be so.

Even if we become enlightened, we can only divulge certain information to the people around us, because some of the knowledge we have is reserved purely for ourselves. If we do attempt to explain it to others they could either, fail to understand, ridicule us for our peculiar beliefs, become angry, or dramatically change the courses of their lives for the wrong reasons, because of what we have disclosed to them, rather than through making their own choices. Having awareness is a very sacred thing and we can only raise our awareness when we are in an appropriate position to do so, when we will use the knowledge wisely.

When your awareness starts to expand treasure the insights you are given, for they will help you to fulfil your true purpose for being on earth and they will guide you through life, furnishing you with strength and determination. Some of your insights will make you utterly jubilant and others will make you desperately sad, because the world offers pain as well as beauty. When you can see the bigger picture, you will become healthily detached from what is happening around you. You will be unwaveringly focused on your path and fulfilling your earthbound duties. The more responsible and aware you become, the more responsibility and hard work you are given, along with a heightened spiritual growth and understanding. Everything you have to do on your journey will be entirely worthwhile.

The real beauty of raised awareness is the ability to see all the changes in your life as sacred blessings, rather than troublesome sacrifices. It really is astonishing to be able to understand why the Universe operates in certain ways, why certain events take place and why you are here. Eventually, you will reach a point where you have no more questions to ask, because you will realise that you have all the answers you could ever need. This is real awareness and it will change your life forever, if you can manage to achieve it in this lifetime.

The exercise below is called Expanding Awareness and will dramatically help you in finding a higher state of consciousness. The Light used in this exercise, will draw your spiritual body through outer space and towards the heavens, where you will be able to see the world down below you from a completely different perspective. The splendour of the Light around you, whether you name that Light God or otherwise, will fill you with unconditional love and when you are at the right place on your journey, it will fill you with wisdom and awareness of yourself and the Universe you inhabit.

Your stresses and worries should begin to evaporate, allowing you to climb over the barriers you have created for yourself in life, to become a much happier, freer and more enlightened being. With your head immersed way up in outer space, you will objectively observe the human beings below frantically running around in their daily lives and you will view their actions from a Universally aware vantage point.

Finally, you will retain your head in this high vantage point and your feet rooted to the ground, so that in all situations in your life you may be able to witness the bigger picture, the true Universal reality of all situations. As you begin to do this, you will grow even more as a human and as a spiritual being.

Exercise

Expanding Awareness

1. Seat yourself down, on a chair, with your feet planted on the ground. Make sure your back is straight. Place your left palm at the back of your head, covering the base of your skull and place your right palm at the front of your head, over your forehead (Fig 13.1).

Fig 13.1

2. Breathe in slowly, through your nose for a count of four. Hold your breath for a count of four, then breathe out through your mouth for a count of four, hold for four, repeating the breathing process until you feel relaxed.

3. Close your eyes and visualise your whole body and the whole room engulfed in beautiful bright white Light. Breathe slowly and deeply without counting.

4. Visualise the Light in the room, expanding upwards towards the sky and towards outer space. As the Light stretches towards the sky visualise the Light pulling you upwards with it, so your spiritual body is getting taller and taller. The Light pulls you to the top of the ceiling,

through the roof to the sky, then through the sky into outer space.

5. As you get taller, be aware of what is going on around you, see the tops of trees below you and birds flying free in the sky. See beautiful white clouds float past you. See the world get smaller below you. As you enter space, look around you at the beautiful bright stars and galaxies. Allow yourself to be mesmerised by what is happening around you.

6. As you travel through space, look upwards and see above you a beautiful bright white Light, so bright that you almost can't look at it. Be amazed and overjoyed by the Light you see. Feel and visualise yourself getting closer and closer to this Light.

7. Just as you are about to enter the Light, silently say to yourself, or out loud, "Please allow me to enter the realm of pure Light that I may see what the world tries to hide." Follow this by saying, "Please allow me to grow and see the world as it stands and the Life inside of me."

8. Visualise yourself entering the pure white beautiful Light and feel yourself being engulfed by pure unconditional love. Feel all your worries disintegrate, as you experience the bliss of being surrounded by nothing but beauty and love in its purest form. Remain encircled in the beautiful white Light for between five minutes and one hour (or more if you want!)

9. After you have enjoyed being part of this wonderful Light, look down below you. See yourself taller and bigger spiritually and look at all the people below you, running around with their hectic lifestyles and worrying

about Universally trivial matters. Feel glad that you have taken the chance to rise above this and grow spiritually.

10. Silently say to yourself, or out loud, "I thank the Light of the Universe for allowing me to grow; I will stay standing tall, so that I may truly know." Follow this by saying, "Let my head remain firmly in the Light with my feet planted on the ground, that I may bridge heaven and earth."

11. Take a deep breath in, filling your stomach and lungs with air and breathe the Light inside your tall spiritual body. Become aware of your feet touching the ground and your middle fingers meeting each other. Feel the sensations of them touching.

12. Feel your feet against the floor and become aware of all the sensations this brings, of your toes, balls of your feet and heels meeting the ground. This should bring your awareness back to your surroundings.

13. Place your hands in gassho (prayer position) with your hands in front of your chest and bow to the Universe.

(N.B. If your arms get tired during this exercise then place them back in gassho (prayer position) in front of your chest.)

Chapter Fourteen

Being Love

One of the foremost pre-requisites of attaining enlightenment is the ability to love all living things, unconditionally. Human beings tend to have countless problems with understanding and being unconditional love. Those who believe that they are offering unconditional love are often very mistaken, confusing earthly love for spiritual love. Furthermore, the word love in itself creates a plethora of unresolved ambiguities. The love, we frequently recognise here on earth, is nothing like the love God has for us and is not in the least bit comparable.

Language, as ever, is inept at realising the reality of the concept. We use the word love so readily, in so many differing circumstances, that it seems to have lost value in the twenty-first century. Some people will pronounce without thought or emotion, "I love chocolate" or "I love my house" or "I love making money." We sign our letters "with love from" or in the case of many self-proclaimed spiritual people "with love and Light." These uses of the word are liberal and largely without any real meaning or purpose. Even when people claim to love someone else, it frequently comes with strict restrictions of a conditional nature. They may proclaim that the contrary is true, but then suddenly, their partners or friends or mothers will do something that leads them to cast doubt upon their love and sometimes this leads to irrational behaviour.

Many people tell their spouses that they will love them infinitely and at some point circumstances prevail that shatter that bond. Perhaps at the time, the words were spoken with genuine sincerity or perhaps in certain situations the words were said without real forethought. In the majority of cases, people's love has strings attached, based on a whole bundle of 'ifs.' If they do this or that for us we will love them. Human love is all too often, fleeting and qualified.

There are individuals who have no comprehension of love in any way, shape or form. They have never loved anyone and thus, will thoughtlessly abuse any living thing without any remorse or an afterthought. Those who commit atrocities such as attacking someone recklessly in the street, in a number of cases will have no concept of love whatsoever, either due to their upbringing or an innate lack of human compassion and spirituality within them. People who have never been shown unconditional love are less likely to be able to display it to anyone else. If you do not *know* love, it is hard *to* love.

With spiritual growth and a greater understanding of our higher selves and the Universe comes a heightened ability to love unconditionally. This is a love that knows no bounds. It is caring but detached and honest, yet firm. This love really **is** eternal and does not depend on a variety of factors and circumstances. Unconditional love does not mean that we let people take advantage of us or suffer fools gladly. Sometimes, loving people means allowing them to learn trying, painful lessons, standing back and watching them suffer under their own imprudence.

We are all, in a sense, God's children and thus we are disciplined accordingly. As I have said previously, humanity breeds its own suffering and those painful circumstances we go through and watch our close ones endure, are lessons in life to be learned from and cherished. It can be incredibly hard watching loved ones in difficult times, but we need to learn when to step in and help and when to take a step back and let them make their own decisions. Everyone has choices in this life. No one is in a position to take away the choices of others. We can offer general guidance from our own awareness and experiences, we can offer friendship and a listening ear, we can even offer healing but we cannot make people's choices for them. If we do, they will never learn from life because they will never have had to take responsibility for themselves. Thus with unconditional love comes a necessary detachment.

Being detached does not mean that we lack empathy with others, but that we care infinitely more about their soul's well-being than their physical state of being. Think of it as caring in a non-caring way, so that whatever happens to those people, will not affect where you are as a person, physically, emotionally or spiritually. You will always be able to view what happens around you with objectivity, because you won't be drawn in by a physical love that wreaks havoc with your emotions. It necessarily implies an emotional detachment from other people.

When I am working in my Reiki practice I come across many clients who have a range of emotional traumas, painful illnesses and heart wrenching life stories. Throughout each treatment I am empathetic and understanding, I can very often identify with peoples' suffering in life. Yet, at the same time, I am not emotionally drawn into their personal situations. I remain detached and objective, because I would be a poor practitioner, if every time someone came to see me I became immersed in his or her emotional traumas. My detachment allows me to offer an impartial, more intuitive point of view. We all need this impartiality to make healthy choices in life.

In the absence of intuitive insight, emotion will often reign and irrational emotions are not conducive to forming objective opinions. A person may come to my practice telling me how much everyone else has ruined his or her life, but as a professional I have to take into account the bigger picture and the wider circumstances surrounding these feelings. When the client leaves, regardless of how benevolent I have been during the treatment, I do not dwell on their lives and emotional traumas. I simply get on with my own life. If we are constantly being drawn into other people's battles, we will be incessantly pulled in all different directions and find ourselves not only fretting about our own lives, but everyone else's as well. If this happens we can become physically and emotionally drained, as well as developing health concerns of our own. We cannot cultivate our own spiritual growth, if we too involved in other people's dilemmas.

Helping people is vital, but the key is to know how to help people in the best way for them and also to understand that some people *cannot* and *do not* want to be helped.

Loving strangers unconditionally, believe it or not, is often a good deal easier than loving our family, close friends and partners unconditionally, but it is something we should strive to achieve. No one wants to see their close ones in pain and their physical love often clouds their better judgement, but in the long run this is more detrimental to the person than being detached. Short-term pain may be necessary for long-term gain. This is all part of our learning process. We need to be able to stand back and look on objectively in all situations, for our own self-development and the spiritual evolution of those around us. Don't worry if you find this to be challenging at the onset. In time, as you move further along your higher path, you will find it easier to be detached from everyone.

Many individuals feel that our families are our closest bonds, that blood is thicker than water, so to speak. We then feel terribly aggrieved when we have a family that is not very tight knit.

From an energetic and soul perspective, the families we have here may bear no relation whatsoever to our souls. In my opinion, a blood bond is nothing, it is all about the souls that we have a spiritual union with. I believe that over each lifetime our souls inhabit different human bodies and thus, each time we dwell on earth, we have new human families. Our souls may never have even encountered the souls of our families before. We should not rely on a family bond. It is more important for us to be close to God (or the Universe or intuition) and to the souls we are energetically familiar with. We have spiritual and physical families, if you like and our physical families may have journeys and higher paths that are entirely dissimilar to our spiritual families.

With all this said, it becomes far easier to be detached from our physical families. Some people will have spiritual ties with their own family members, but others will not and if the energetic bond is not there, there is no point trying to build on something that does not exist. We should be focusing on our own paths and as along as we are doing this, everything else will fall into place.

I am also a firm believer in soul mates. By this I mean that each one of us is made up of energy, but that energy is not complete and our soul mates form the rest of that energy. Your soul mate could be a partner, mother, friend, brother or even someone you have not even met yet. When you are with your soul mate you feel incredibly happy. They seem to possess the missing elements that you feel you lack within yourself and vice versa. They are in essence, very similar to you and when they are around you, you feel more like yourself. You have a personal closeness with them that you could never have with anyone else. They are the missing piece of your puzzle.

If you discover your soul mate, you will never want to let them go and the love you have for them will be way above and beyond any love that you have for any other person (apart from yourself and God). You will be far closer to your soul mate than your own family (unless they are a member of your family). If you meet your soul mate, embrace them. Soul mates that meet each other in this lifetime are usually meant to be working together on their spiritual journeys. If you feel that unparalleled bond with someone, that is more about a soul connection than anything else, know that they are your soul mate.

There is a misconception, held by some people, that loving unconditionally means that we have to be affable to everyone and like them as human beings. This is not the case. Sometimes, we need to be very stern and forthright. This is far more honest and spiritually minded, than painting on a false smile through gritted teeth. There is no wisdom in insincerity. Just because we love someone unconditionally, whether it is a friend, family member or otherwise, it does not mean that we have to like that person. If people are behaving negatively or in a manner that is contrary to your ethics and spiritual nature, you do not have to be exceedingly nice to them or give them the benefit of the doubt.

With heightened intuition and wisdom, comes a better judge of character and sometimes people are just unpleasant and harmful to us. If this is the case, we need to avoid them or maintain minimal contact, remaining assertive. Don't pretend to like individuals that are downright mean, or feel guilty for having an aversion to them. We can only lie to ourselves. We cannot lie to our higher selves, to God or the Universe.

Some human beings commit brutal injustices and there is no value in us spending our valuable time and energy trying to find something agreeable in their character. Our precious energy should be reserved for those that we do have time for and that have the potential to develop a greater understanding and enhanced spiritual awareness in life. Indeed live and let live or live and let die, let people make their own choices. We are not here to please others. We are here to fulfil our true purpose. Love everyone unconditionally and like those who deserve to be liked.

Loving unconditionally also entails loving every single living thing. All life on this earth is precious. We should love, nurture and care about **all** living creatures, unconditionally. If we can bring ourselves to inflict gratuitous harm on any living creature then we have lost the ability to love unconditionally.

Remember, that everyone on this earth has a purpose for being here and all purposes are equally valid. Whilst some are sent to shed love and Light on the world, others are sent to inflict pain and suffering. Both jobs have equal validity. The right and wrong on a Universal scale, is not the same as we choose to label it here on earth. A murderer, for instance, may well have been sent to earth to commit the very fatal deed they undertook. We may find them contemptible for it, but we have to accept that they fulfilled their darker purpose. This doesn't necessarily mean that all murderers are sent with that purpose as their aim in life, but some beings on this earth are here to do the opposite of what we would call 'good' and their role carries as much weight and worth as anyone else's.

We should carry out the work we were sent to do here and let others carry out their own work, whether we deem it as right, wrong or otherwise. One human being cannot change the fate of the whole world, or deprive the world of its many injustices. They can make a small difference where they are able to and nothing more. Don't waste your time trying to set yourself unrealisable goals of instigating a worldwide spiritual revolution, because not everyone will be willing to change their way of life. Whilst some people will happily open up to their more spiritual and intuitive self, others will never in their whole lifetime wish to, or were never meant to embark upon this journey. Again, allow people to make their own choices by loving them unconditionally.

The exercise below is entitled Allowing Unconditional Love and will help you to initiate a heightened state of being and consciousness, by slowing down your breathing, which will also aid relaxation. In this state, you will become more able to understand the true meaning of unconditional love.

The pink bright Light, in the technique, will fill you with peace, tranquillity and a sense of inner warmth and peace that will radiate throughout your body and beyond. By gently smiling to yourself, you will subconsciously register a state of contentment and a self and Universal acceptance.

With the affirmation, you are committing to loving unconditionally, so that you yourself will become the epitome of love and Light. As the pink Light transforms to a beautiful white Light, your spiritual body will expand as you absorb increasing levels of wisdom and eternal enduring love. Your spiritual body will grow to such an extent that the world will appear to you as a minute dot, symbolising how far you have come from your physical state of existence, to the spiritually aware state you now find yourself in. With your new giant spiritual body, you will be able to fit in heaps more boundless unconditional love that will stay with you, wherever you go in life and beyond.

Try to carry out this exercise between three and five times a week (or more if you can) and let true unconditional love be your guide.

Exercise

Allowing Unconditional Love

1. Sit down comfortably, either on the floor in seiza (on
    your knees with your bottom resting on your heels) or in
    agura (cross-legged) or on a chair. Make sure your back
    is straight. Have your hands palms facing upwards, in
    your lap.

2. Breathe in through your nose slowly, for a count of four
    and breathe out even more slowly through your mouth
    for a count of eight. Try to slow your breathing down to
    five or six breaths per minute. Continue this process for
    between three and fifteen minutes.

3. Visualise the whole room, filled with beautiful bright
    light pink energy. See the energy swirling around the
    room and watch as the pink energy enters your head and
    floats down through your entire body. Visualise your
    body becoming one with the bright light pink energy in
    the room.

4. Gently smile to yourself as you feel the softness and
    serenity of the calming pink energy.

5. Place your hands in gassho (prayer position) in front of
    your chest. Silently say to yourself, or out loud, with
    meaning and purpose, seven times, "I seek to become
    unconditional love so that I may speak the true words of
    the Light above."

6. Visualise the beautiful pink energy that is engulfing your
    body and the room, turning into bright white Light. As
    the Light changes colour, visualise your spiritual body

stretching upwards and outwards so that your spiritual body becomes bigger than the room. See your spiritual body continue to grow and grow, until your body has become so huge that you can no longer see where it begins and where it ends. Visualise that your spiritual body has expanded so much that you can look down and see the earth as a tiny, tiny dot.

7. When you have expanded your spiritual body as much as you can, silently say to yourself, or out loud, with meaning and purpose seven times, "Let my entire being become filled with unconditional love, so that I will know the truth of the Light above."

8. When you have completed this process, repeat steps 3 through to 7, three times (or more if you wish).

9. When you have finished, bow to the Universe.

Chapter Fifteen

Accepting Your Higher Path

Accepting your true purpose for being here is not necessarily an easy task to accomplish. Our most beautiful journey in life can be challenging, trying, lonely at times, sad and deeply life transforming. Humans are prone to disliking change, so the upheaval of turning your whole life around can be a struggle. Despite all this, any grief or suffering you experience in trying to pursue your higher path, is insignificant when you consider the mountain of benefits and the re-connection to your soul. There are no sacrifices involved, only a wonderful life giving, learning and growing process that will ensure your destiny is one of beauty and spiritual triumph, rather than one of pain and misguided searching. There really is no happiness like re-uniting with your soul, discovering and fulfilling your life's purpose and becoming one with yourself and the Universe.

The dawn of the journey is always more troublesome because it can be a time of great confusion and uncertainty, where you are not sure if you are really trusting your intuition or if you are succumbing to your rational mind. The people around you may not be supportive of the changes taking place within you. Indeed, some of them may say that they preferred the way you used to be, because the new more enlightened you is deeply frightening for them. Looking at an enlightened being is like staring into a fountain of truth and those who know and live the truth display it to the world in the glimpse of an eye.

Some people will be instantly drawn to you because of your deep connection, others will look at you and see all the things they dislike about themselves, and they will not thank you for it. This is just the way of the world. As I have said before, we are not here to please others we are here to fulfil our purposes. In time you will learn to stop worrying about what other people think of you.

Accepting your higher path fully means gathering the strength to walk that path, regardless of any given situations you are in and your external environment. It means being the **real** you, wherever you are, possessing such a strong belief in your path that no man or woman can shake you from it. This acceptance should not be with resentment or wistfulness, but with an utter determination and resolution to complete your true purpose.

Sometimes, it can be a mammoth struggle to accept your higher path, because it presents so many challenges and increasing levels of responsibility, but remember always that it is so utterly rewarding above and beyond all that. There may be days when you feel tired, when you would rather go back to bed and sleep for an aeon and when your path seems an impossible trial. In reality, we are never given anything that we cannot handle on our paths. We are much stronger than we ever dare to realise and when we do dare, we achieve better and greater things.

Lack of acceptance causes colossal conflicts within us that are not readily reconciled, our heads pound daily with a symphony of differing thoughts and contradictory messages. It is only upon acceptance of our true purpose that we can truly gain the clarity we need, to work towards being the truth and possessing real wisdom. Our inner conflicts, our inner saboteurs that seek desperately to turf us off our higher paths, halt our development and in time if left to reign, can drag us off our divine paths completely.

Acceptance of your true purpose may seem hard but the reality is that it is so very simple, just accept. Stop for a second, silence the conflicting voices within you for a moment of peace and you will see that only your higher path can bring you the true fulfilment you need and wish for in life. The rest is peripheral and can only bring temporary relief and false contentment.

Anyone who is bold enough to say that following your higher path is effortless is a liar. If it were all plain sailing we would not learn real lessons. The trials of life and the trials of our higher paths are astounding gifts that light our way, if we dare to see that Light. Some people believe or perhaps hope, that once they have found their calling they will embark upon a fairy tale lifestyle, but everyone knows that fairytales are make believe. Yet in saying that, the truth and the course of our higher paths are exquisite, more so than a human mind could ever imagine because we are all well and truly trussed, limited by our humanity and we are set free by our spiritual nature, our glorious souls.

So I beseech you, when you find the magnificence that is your true purpose for being on this earth, your higher path, embrace it with all your might, hold it dear to you and walk that path with faith, humility and complete gratitude. You will be tested, we always are, but when you prove yourself, your spiritual development will be unstoppable and enlightenment will be but a few footsteps away.

The technique for this chapter is entitled Accepting Higher Path Gracefully and will help you to acknowledge your true purpose. It can be hard to do this in trying situations and sometimes we need to boost our waning courage and conviction. This technique will help you to do this, if practised regularly. Use it especially at times when you feel your morale is flagging, or when you feel that you are drifting away from your higher path.

A huge part of this exercise involves clearing negative energy, especially emotional traumas from your chest area. These traumas can block your personal growth and muffle the voice of your soul, your intuition. The colours of the rainbow are breathed in individually, followed by pure white Light. The reason behind this is that I believe that each colour of the rainbow, from red through to violet, has a specific frequency, which corresponds to the optimum frequencies of cells, organs and even emotions within the physical body. These healing energies will help any frequency imbalances within you to be addressed. The white Light incorporates the entire spectrum of frequencies, offering a high frequency spiritual healing.

The removal of negative energies from your body and being will prevent your life's traumas from obscuring your clarity of thought and vision. As you breathe out in this exercise, the negative energy will pour out of your mouth to be sent to God, or the Universe to convert to positive energy.

Once you have created in effect a blank sheet of paper to work from, you will infuse your body with the affirmation that you accept your higher path and by doing this you will be able to grow and develop yourself spiritually. Try to practise this exercise at least three times a week.

Exercise

Accepting Higher Path Gracefully

1. Sit down comfortably either on the floor in seiza (on your knees with your bottom resting on your heels) or in agura (cross-legged) or on a chair. Make sure your back is straight. Have your hands palms facing upwards, in your lap.

2. As you breathe in very slowly and deeply through your nose, visualise that the air you breathe in is a red Light (or energy), see this Light enter your nostrils, travel down your windpipe and fill your lungs with beautiful red Light. Expand your lungs as much as you can, as you do this. As you breathe out through your mouth, visualise black negative energy in your lungs rising into your throat and pouring out from your mouth. Continue this process for a couple of minutes. Try to slow your breathing down to five or six breaths per minute.

3. When you have finished silently say to yourself, or out loud, "I pray that the Universe may convert the negative energy I have expelled to positive Light."

4. Repeat step 2, followed by 3, replacing red Light with orange Light.

5. Repeat steps 2 and 3 with yellow Light.

6. Repeat steps 2 and 3 with green Light.

7. Repeat steps 2 and 3 with blue Light.

8. Repeat steps 2 and 3 with indigo Light.

9. Repeat steps 2 and 3 with violet Light.

10. Repeat steps 2 and 3 with white Light.

11. Place your hands in gassho (prayer position) in front of your chest. Silently say to yourself, or out loud, with meaning and purpose five times, "I accept my higher path on earth; I learn to grow and grow to learn. Let the Light of the Universe be my guide."

12. Repeat steps 2 and 3 with white Light.

13. Silently say to yourself, or out loud, with meaning and purpose, five times, "I gain all that I could ever need by accepting my higher path and growing with my path gracefully."

14. Carry out steps 11 through to 13 between one and three times.

15. When you have finished, bow to the Universe.

Chapter Sixteen

Being Truth

Naturally following: balance, awareness, unconditional love and acceptance of your higher path, is the ability to live or epitomise the truth. This is more than a knowing, it involves **right living** and **right thinking** in every area of your life. Your thoughts and your words have power and as an enlightened being, you should not be generating destructive thoughts or sending out negative energy. Every step you take in life breeds a consequence and therefore, each precious step requires forethought. You should be at a stage where you do not need to ask if what you are doing is the right thing to do, because instinctively, intuitively, you know without even pausing to contemplate, you know precisely what you have to do and without question or query you actually go ahead and do it.

The reality lies before you as you look upon the world around you. You bear witness to the reality **you** discovered from your work in previous chapters and now you become real yourself, for all that went before your learning is like a dream. This is the dream that most people live on a day-to-day basis. Those still asleep may scoff at your behaviour and deem you to be daft and senseless but the reality is quite different, they walk with their eyes closed and live without Living. You have awoken from your slumber and you live the truth, you became the truth when you set your soul free. Do not be afraid if others do not see as you do, some people will always be blind to the real truth of the Universe, they will always be intoxicated by their physical wants and desires. Let them be, they have made their choices. Others will look at you and will want to know what it is that you see and they too, like you, will search for their higher self, for wisdom and veracity.

How do you 'be the truth?' Quite simply, by always doing the right things for your higher self and soul, whatever those things happen to be, by walking your path steadfast, regardless of how other people perceive you. In effect you are saying, "This is my path and I **will** walk it, forever!"

This shouldn't be mistaken for a wilful determination to do what you want in life (unless what you want happens to be everything that your higher path entails.) This is not about getting your own way all the time and trampling over your soul. You can only become the truth when you are ready for it, when you have surrendered to your intuition and your true purpose. Surrendering to your whims, fancies and emotional crutches does not count. An enlightened soul has come to want what they need, rather than what they were never meant to have. We are often told that we can have anything we want, but this is an illusion. We can only have what we want if it is within divine will and there are always consequences.

Your true happiness and sense of inner peace and well-being will rapidly increase, as you start to become the real you in every aspect of your life. There are always times when it is difficult to speak your mind, or when you hold back from saying your piece, because the fear weighs you down.

This fear will dissipate, as you become the truth, for you will realise that you have nothing left to fear, as far as your path is concerned.

The beauty of becoming more aware is the knowing you foster within, that no matter what happens to you in life, everything will be ok for you. You cannot really be harmed when you walk your true path. People can try to push you off it, or ridicule you, or even damage you physically, but they cannot steal your freedom, something that if they continue to behave the way they are, they will never ever have.

At this time, try not to scatter 'what ifs?' around you, as they will form obstacles and fuel the development of fears. If your higher self instructs you to "walk with me this way," then do it. Do not put unnecessary barriers in front of you or else you will trip up and lose direction. In essence, just go with the flow of your intuition. If any questions about your path crop up, ask God, or the Universe, or your intuition, but don't become incredibly frustrated and impudent if an answer is not given. Patience is a virtue. All will become apparent in good time. We are given answers when we need them and in reality we have all the answers we could ever possibly need.

Your plain, simple and honest living will help to guide you in life and keep you on your higher path. Your pursuit of the truth will illuminate your passage to freedom. Your living of the truth will enliven you and you will know what it really means to Live. Peace can be yours if you become the truth.

The exercise below, entitled Your True Self, will help you to develop your confidence in your own wisdom and allow you to realise your spiritual potential. The connection between your physical and spiritual self will become stronger, so that your three bodies (physical, emotional and spiritual) can join together and become one. That way, you will always be heading in one direction and each of your bodies will be leading you in that direction. Your emotional and physical bodies will not try to drag you off on different routes. They will be a part of the whole truth that you have become.

This exercise will also aid you in speaking the truth to others who are ready to hear it. Some will never be ready, but those who are will benefit from what you have to say. This doesn't mean that you can boss people around, simply that your inner truth will radiate from your spoken words. Your words have power, use them.

By bowing to the Universe in this following technique, you are demonstrating humility in the face of God's or the Universe's wisdom. Never forget that enlightened souls are truly humble, for we never stop learning no matter how wise we become. Practise this exercise daily.

Fig 16.1

Exercise

Your True Self

1. Sit down comfortably either on the floor in seiza (on your knees with your bottom resting on your heels) or in agura (cross-legged) or on a chair. Make sure your back is straight. Place your hands in gassho (prayer position) in front of your chest.

2. Breathe in and out very slowly and deeply through your nose, noticing the feeling of the air entering and exiting your nostrils. Focus on this for a few minutes to help you relax.

3. Place your right palm over your navel and your left palm over your forehead (Fig 16.1). Feel the air enter into and leave your stomach as you breathe in and out for a few seconds.

4. Silently say to yourself, or out loud, with meaning and purpose, for between three and fifteen minutes, "I am my true higher self, I am confident being me, I will speak the truth to all those who wish to hear me."

5. Place your hands back in gassho (prayer position) in front of your chest. Bow gently forward before returning to an upright position and silently saying to yourself, or out loud, with meaning and purpose, seven times, "I bow to the wisdom of the Light of the Universe. I bow to the wisdom of my higher self."

6. When you have finished take a deep breath in and out, through your nose, then bow to the Universe again.

Being Wise, Having Faith

Introduction to Part Five

"We cannot take wisdom for granted. It is earned from living a spiritual life and comes from within those who truly Live. The wise have faith because they know what most choose not to know and their faith is permanent. If you have wisdom and faith, then cherish it always for you are truly blessed."

If you have come this far and achieved the other goals, you are in a fantastic place. The knowledge of the Universe is whirring around your brain and you can feel deep within you that so many positive changes have taken place already. You should be feeling much more at peace with yourself and have a higher understanding of the world you inhabit and the Universe that envelops that world. You should be at a place where you are brimming with wonderment, amazement, unconditional love and a real sense of accomplishment, and your enthusiasm for fulfilling your true purpose and potential should be at its all time high.

Pride should fill your entire being, not foolish pride but a dignity and self-respect that radiates within you and through to every single thing you do in life. Be happy that you have achieved this, be humble and willing to learn the greater faith and wisdom that is to come, be vigilant for those who seek to sweep the rug from under your feet. Fulfilling all this will serve you well in life.

Your efforts at self-improvement and self-awareness, if maintained, will ensure that greater wisdom becomes yours. As your frequency elevates, through your hard work and you tread towards enlightenment, your spiritual body will stretch for the heavens and you will be discover a whole new realm of inner insight and knowledge.

You may be tempted to holler from the rooftops and declare all you have discovered to everyone who dares to pass you by, but this would be incredibly foolhardy. This is where real wisdom comes in. There are people who make allegedly amazing discoveries about their own spirituality and they take these discoveries to be the truths of all humankind. In some ways, it is similar to someone presuming that because they are of an elder generation they are wiser and thus by that token, they push their life's experiences on all those around them. This lacks deep intuitive insight.

Wisdom comes from learning from our lessons in life and knowing whom to distribute that wisdom to and when to do it, if at all. Not to mention, that we are all given very personal insights that apply only to our own circumstances. Remember again, that everyone on this earth is different and we all have different purposes in life, no one is better than the other but each is unique. Wisdom is also about living every day of your life, in the way that is right for your spiritual journey. Walk your path with understanding, foresight and a willingness to learn.

The first section of this chapter will discuss in more detail the wisdom needed to pursue a path to enlightenment. Wisdom is often not what it is assumed to be and knowing the difference between genuine intuitive insight and the musings of a consciously mediated mind, is a key factor in your self-development and spiritual path.

We cannot possess wisdom if we do not have complete faith in our higher paths and ourselves. Doubt and hesitation about what we are here to do suggests a lack of faith and a mistrusting of our intuition.

Our intuition is always correct. Our other human faculties can fail us, but not our intuition. It is our greatest gift, our connection to God or the Universe and the source of all our wisdom.

Never let anyone make you question your intuition. People can play games with your mind and they can beguile you, lull you into a false sense of security and trip you up, but if you always abide by your intuition, they can never do you any real spiritual harm. If anyone dares ever to tell you that intuition can be mistaken, then they really are not worth listening to. Have faith in yourself, have faith in what you know to be true, regardless of what those around you may say to you. Certainly do not try and force your beliefs on others, but if your higher self, your intuition tells you "hang on a minute, this person isn't telling the truth," then have faith in your own inner wisdom.

Don't be thrown off your higher path in life because of the mumblings of a few people who are not at the same point spiritually as you are. The stronger our faith is in our higher selves and in God (if you believe in God) the more enlightened we become. Our faith carries us through all the trials in our lives and helps us to stick like glue to what we know to be true. Losing faith is like experiencing bereavement, finding faith is worth more than all the money in the world.

The second part of this chapter will discuss faith in more detail and provide techniques to ensure that your faith stays strong in all that you do, in fulfilling your true purpose.

Wisdom and faith will change your life forever and you will never look back and wish you could be anywhere else but where you are now. The journey on earth is magnificent, if we tread each step in the right direction. Our time here is just the beginning, a seed planted in the earth just shooting through the soil, and we plant each seed and we choose if that plant flourishes or dies, so we must choose wisely. Always tread carefully and make the choices that take you to a higher level.

Chapter Seventeen

Being Wise

Wisdom is an extremely misinterpreted trait. People make all sorts of assumptions about what wisdom naturally implies. These assumptions, which are often misguided, result in lots of lost individuals wandering the planet looking for answers in all the wrong places, or, simply not looking for any answers at all because they think they have them all already. We are all learning and however wise we become, the learning process continues, for as long as we are here.

First of all, spiritual wisdom has nothing to do with our intelligence quota or our intellectual ability. You can be a member of Mensa, with an IQ of 170, who has read nearly every book in existence, but this does not *automatically* mean that you are wise. Wisdom is derived from intuition, not from human intellectualism. There is quite a number of what we would denote as 'intelligent' people inhabiting the earth and many of them probably lead irresponsible lifestyles. Having a super powered memory and a problem solving brain does not intrinsically mean that someone embraces the concept of right living, right thinking and Universal understanding. Of course, there will be highly intelligent people that are wise with it, but this is not by virtue of their intelligence. Their wisdom is born out of intuition.

Some of the cruellest people on this earth are the most intelligent with highly calculating minds, but they are not wise! If you do not know your higher self, if you cannot hear the voice of your soul then how can you possibly claim to have wisdom? Only when we open up to our higher selves, either consciously, subconsciously, or both, can we garner the knowledge of the Universe and of our deepest truths. Book smarts do not intrinsically breed enlightenment. We should only believe something if it concurs with our intuition, not simply because it has been said or written, even if it has been said or written prolifically.

Secondly, do not assume someone is wise just because they pronounce their own spirituality. Wisdom comes from within us, not from external sources. Anyone can claim to be spiritual, without a thought for all the necessary implications. The word in solitary is meaningless, unless the individual has a really firm grasp on the concept and lives their entire life in a spiritual way. Dabbling in tarot cards, angels, runes etc, or being a holistic practitioner, or claiming to be a guru does not automatically mean that any wisdom or intuition is involved. Words are empty unless they backed up by actions.

The wise do not take people for what they say they are but for how they know them to be. Of course, anyone can read books or listen to people and gain certain insights from them, but it is vital to learn the difference between being presented with real intuition and being presented with the workings of the mind or regurgitated material. Take what you need from the books that you read, take what you need from the words that you hear, but ignore all that does not resonate with your intuition. Believe only that which is true in the things that you hear, not everything that you hear. Trust only in what you know can be trusted, not in everything that desires your trust. Humans are prone to jumping on bandwagons. Always use your intuition in every area of your life.

True wisdom is so rare, but so magnificent and we all possess wisdom within us waiting to be set free. You will find that as your inner wisdom proliferates, the words that pour forth from your mouth do not seem to be your own, but those from a higher source. When we are deeply connected to our intuition we have a higher awareness and the words we utter come from God or if you prefer, the Universe, or our higher self.

Sometimes, an individual will ask you a challenging question about life and for a split second you will think, "I really don't know how I am going to answer this." Suddenly, your intuition will kick in and a stream of profound insights will come gushing forth from your lips. Afterwards, you will probably find yourself thinking, "I do not remember a word that I said to that person," but you will know that you spoke the truth and that you said exactly what you needed to say.

When we are connected to our higher selves, we are always given answers when we need them and the wise know how to use these answers in the best possible way to suit their higher paths in life.

Those who possess true wisdom of thought and action do not brag relentlessly about their life's experiences, or try to force anyone into adopting their point of view. This is because the wise know that everybody will listen at a time that is right for them, or they may never listen, but we can only offer ears to listen and general advice. We cannot take anyone's lessons away from them, or force our beliefs onto others. Neither, can we change the whole world as I have mentioned before, we can only help those who are destined to cross our paths. The wise are realistic and understand completely their limitations on this earth, as well as their potential successes.

I will say yet again, right thinking, right living. Those with insight practise what they preach, because they believe in what they know to be true and tenaciously follow their path. They do this with great resolve in the pursuit of far reaching truths and with determination to experience and show the meaning of true freedom. The wise know the wise when they encounter each other and can establish the difference between wise men and fools.

There are two techniques outlined for this chapter, entitled Shaping Wisdom and Being Wisdom respectively. The first method will help you to delve into your inner knowledge and use the wisdom you discover to direct you through life.

The patting of various parts of the body, utilised in this technique, will gently open you up to your higher self, your deepest intuition and the Universe or God. It will also help you to focus and gain real inner clarity that will then exude from you as you practise this exercise on a regular basis.

By allowing Light to permeate your entire body, you are developing a firmer connection with your higher self and allowing healing to take place within you that will free you from your emotional traumas. This exercise should help your actions to follow your thoughts and words, so that you can truly be insightful and maintain this level of awareness. Try to practise this technique at least three times a week.

The second exercise, Being Wisdom will allow truth to emanate from you, so that regardless of any difficulties or challenging questions you are presented with, you will always maintain confidence and a deep intuitive connection. When the right words need to be said, they will naturally flow from your mouth and you will let them do so without questioning or letting thought take over from intuition. The breathing exercise will calm you and clear your mind.

The red Light surrounding you and filling your body will create self-belief and help you to trust in what you know. The white Light will be a beacon, to help drive you correctly through your life, and the affirmations will sink into your body, mind and soul as you let the Universe and your inner insights become your greatest guide to all thoughts and all actions. Again, try to practise this exercise at least three times a week.

Fig 17.1   Fig 17.2

Exercise

Shaping Wisdom

1. Sit down comfortably, either on the floor in seiza (on your knees with your bottom resting on your heels) or in agura (cross-legged) or on a chair. Make sure your back is straight. Place your hands in gassho (prayer position) in front of your chest.

2. Breathe in and out very slowly and deeply through your nose, noticing the feeling of the air entering and exiting your nostrils. Focus on this for a few minutes to help you relax. Allow your hands to drop down by your side.

3. Using your right hand, pat the crown of your head three times (Fig 17.1).

4. Using your right hand, pat your forehead three times (Fig 17.2).

5. Using your right hand, pat your throat three times (Fig 17.3).

6. Using your left hand pat the top of your chest at the centre 3 times (Fig 17.4).

7. Using your left hand, pat the bottom of your chest at the centre three times (Fig 17.5).

8. Using your left hand, pat your navel area three times (Fig 17.6).

Fig 17.3

Fig 17.4

Fig 17.5

Fig 17.6

9. Place your hands back in gassho (prayer position) in front of your chest. Visualise white Light filling your entire body and see that Light radiating out from your body and expanding until the Light fills the whole room.

10. Visualise Light coming down from space, as far up as the eye can see. Allow that Light, as it enters the room, to merge with the Light you are radiating outwards from yourself.

11. Maintain this visualisation and silently say to yourself, or out loud, with meaning and purpose, three times, "May my actions breed wisdom and life within me, that my truest nature will be set free."

12. Using steps 3 through to 8, repeat the affirmation, patting the relevant area **after** you have completed the affirmation three times.

13. At the end, bow to the Universe in gassho (prayer position) with your hands in front of your chest.

Being Wisdom

1. Sit down comfortably either on the floor in seiza (on your knees with your bottom resting on your heels) or in agura (cross-legged) or on a chair. Make sure your back is straight. Place your hands in gassho (prayer position) in front of your chest.

2. Breathe in slowly and deeply through your nose, taking as much air in as you can. When your lungs feel full, try to take in a little bit more air and push it into your abdomen. Breathe out through your mouth very, very slowly forming an 'O' shape with your mouth, as you do so. When your lungs feel empty, try to breathe out a little bit more expelling air from your abdomen. Continue with this breathing technique for a few minutes or until you feel completely relaxed.

3. Place both your palms over your ears (Fig 17.7) and visualise red Light coming down from the furthest reaches of space and filling up the room and your entire body, allow yourself to feel safe and cosy within the Light.

4. With your palms still over your ears, silently say to yourself, with meaning and purpose, seventeen times, "Wisdom exudes from my very core. The Light within me is my guiding law."

5. Place your palms at the back of your head, cupping the base of your skull (Fig 17.8) and repeat the affirmation from step 4, seventeen times.

6. Place one hand on your solar plexus region and the other over your navel (Fig 17.9) and repeat the affirmation from step 4, seventeen times.

7. Visualise the red Light turning into white Light and then being swallowed up into the centre of your body, so a big ball of white Light is glowing inside of you and the room has now returned to its usual state.

8. Silently say to yourself, with meaning and purpose, three times, "I endeavour to be wise in every way, guide me to wisdom in the Way of the Universe, and Light my path to walk with me."

9. When you have finished, bow to the Universe in gassho (prayer position) with your hands in front of your chest.

Fig 17.7

Fig 17.8

Fig 17.9

Chapter Eighteen

Having Faith

Many people wish they had more faith, yet it is something that appears to be elusive to the many. There are individuals who have always had faith throughout their lives, those who had faith and then lost it, leading them to question the very core of their beliefs and those who never had faith and who cannot understand faith in any way, shape or form.

We cannot successfully traverse through life without having faith in our intuition, in ourselves and in the reality of what we can achieve. Without faith we feel hopeless, lacking in direction and we meander through this life wondering what went wrong and why we didn't achieve our full potential. Life can be a struggle and it is not always easy in the face of certain situations to maintain your convictions, but faith is essential for spiritual growth and personal development.

As you become more connected to your higher self, as you heal all of your emotional traumas, you will find it much easier to retain your faith and believe in yourself, regardless of circumstance. We all possess strength and courage, if we look inside ourselves hard enough. It is just a matter of being able to find that courage and then using that courage in your daily life.

Becoming more enlightened doesn't always make for an easy path in life, but it makes for a much more rewarding, satisfying and soul-nurturing path, than any other options you might choose from. We all inevitably, find ourselves mired in circumstances beyond our control. The key is to be able to adapt to those circumstances, have faith that everything will be as it should be and to keep looking within for the answers, knowing that those answers we wish for will come when we need them. If we lack faith, we are always going to stall our progress because we will form needless obstacles and escape routes, when we should really be looking towards the positive lifestyle changes we could be initiating.

Once you are truly governed by your intuition, you will find that with each new trial in life your faith grows. Do not worry about losing your faith, just do what you know you should be doing, follow your intuition and your true purpose and everything else will fall into place.

Losing faith is a form of bereavement, for those who had and then lost it, finding faith again will be an amazing triumph and the faith you cultivate when you are connected to your soul, is so much greater than any faith you may have had previously, because it comes from true insight.

I would like to be able to say that establishing faith is a breeze, but it requires a lot of hard work and dedication. The hard work we put in is what makes the discovery of faith so intensely rewarding. I lost my faith for a long time and it was exceptionally difficult to recapture. I had lost all confidence in myself, in my intuition, in God, even though deep down the niggling feeling that God existed did not abate. When I finally rediscovered my faith I was both elated and terrified. This fear was not of being punished by God, but guilt for the way I had lived my life. I felt as if my eyes had been opened and I could see that before my revelation I had been living in the dark. I was behaving in a way that was not the real me. I had done things that I was not at all proud of.

It was not long before I realised that I had nothing to fear, I just had to change my life for the better and accept and follow my path. Once I managed to achieve this my faith grew stronger every day. Life threw trials at me but I did not lose faith. I came out the other side a more intuitive, self-confident and happier person. I had fostered self-belief where before I'd had none. I felt a love like no other, surrounding me wherever I went. I allowed God and the Universe to guide me. My life became infinitely more rewarding and purposeful and I had answers that I could only ever have dreamed of in the past.

I implore you to find faith in yourself, the Universe and in God, if you believe in God. Faith is so liberating and when it is sincerely yours, no one will be able to take it away from you. You know the truth, you have faith and you have intuition. The beauty of your journey is discovering this and you will find nothing else in life to be so magnificent and so worthwhile. Walk your path with devotion and commitment. It will set you free.

There are two exercises below, one entitled Fostering Faith and the other, Keeping Faith. The first method, Fostering Faith will help you to expand your strength of conviction, by allowing you to open yourself up to your inner knowledge and to the knowledge of the Universe.

By focusing on your middle fingers in prayer position and engulfing yourself in Light, you will centre yourself and foster the further growth of your intuition. The affirmations will build on your self-belief and trust in the Universe, to guide you and keep you safe.

By prostrating yourself, you are submitting yourself to the wisdom, power, and love of God, or the Universe and recognising that, as part of God's creation you are a wonderful soul, who is connected to everyone and everything. In doing this, you are additionally offering gratitude for the faith that resides within you and develops with each second of each new day. When you express faith in your heart, body and spirit, you are deepening the connection of your body, mind and soul and allowing your intuition to permeate the essence of your being. In this way, your physical and emotional bodies will be one with your spiritual body. Practise this exercise at least four times a week.

The second exercise, Keeping Faith will ensure that whatever situation you are presented with, you will react with steadfast resolve and never let anyone or anything make you question the convictions you know to be true.

As you place your palms over your eyes, you will begin to experience deep healing relaxation and the rainbow of Light spiralling through you will allow your soul to reach higher into the heavens, as your body heals on a physical and emotional level.

The affirmation is a demonstration of your personal commitment to your faith in yourself and the Universe. With every new hand position you will push the affirmation into your body, mind and spirit, so that the words are not just spoken but truly believed and understood.

Finally, you will express gratitude for the Light within you that allows you to fulfil your true higher purpose in life and gratitude to God or the Universe, for **everything** that has every happened to you in your life. Practise this exercise every day if you can. The results will be worth the endeavour.

Exercise

Fostering Faith

1. Sit down comfortably on the floor in seiza (on your knees with your bottom resting on your heels). Make sure your back is straight. Place your hands in gassho (prayer position) in front of your chest.

2. Direct your eyes downwards, to your palms and allow them to focus on your two middle fingers as they meet (Fig 18.1). Feel these two fingers pressed against each other.

3. As you continue focusing on your middle fingers, breathe in very slowly through your nose, for a count of four and out through your mouth for a count of four. Continue this process for between three and fifteen minutes, until your feel more calm and centred.

4. Return your head to an upright position and focus your attention on the feeling of your palms pressed together. Bring your hands still in gassho against the centre of your chest, so your thumbs are pressed against your sternum (Fig 18.2). Breathe in slowly, through your nose and out through your mouth as you do this.

5. Visualise a bright white Light, so bright it is almost impossible to look at, coming down through space as far up as the eye can see. See the Light enter the crown of your head from above, like a radiant beam and allow the Light to enter your body from your head through to the tips of your toes.

6. Silently say to yourself or out loud, with meaning and purpose, seven times, "I have faith in myself to set my intuition free, I have faith in the Light of the Universe that has faith in me."

7. Raise your palms still in gassho straight above your head (Fig 18.3).

8. Turn your palms so they face outwards, away from your body (Fig 18.4).

9. Prostrate yourself on the floor, with your knees bent and your body face down, with your forehead rested on the floor and your arms stretched out above your head (Fig 18.5). Have your palms resting lightly on the floor.

10. Silently say to yourself or out loud, with meaning and purpose, seven times, "My faith grows like a newly planted seed. I have faith in the Light of the Universe that has faith in me."

11. Raise yourself off the ground to an upright position. Place your hands back in gassho, with your arms outstretched above your head (Fig 18.3).

12. Bring your palms back down in gassho position to your chest.

13. Repeat steps 6 through to 12 between three and nine times.

14. Silently say to yourself, or out loud, with meaning and purpose, "I have faith in my heart" then move your hands in gassho to your stomach (Fig 18.6) and continue, "I have faith in my body," then move your hands in gassho to the middle of your forehead (your third eye)

(18.7) and continue, "I have faith in my spirit to fulfil my higher path."

15. When you have finished, bow to the Universe in gassho (prayer position) with your hands in front of your chest.

Fig 18.5

Fig 18.6   Fig 18.7

Keeping Faith

1. Sit down comfortably, either on the floor in seiza (on your knees with your bottom resting on your heels) or in agura (cross-legged) or on a chair. Make sure your back is straight. Place your hands in gassho (prayer position) in front of your chest.

2. Breathe in for a count of seven and out for a count of seven, slowly and deeply through your nose. Fill your abdomen with air first, then your lungs, as you breathe in and then empty your lungs and your abdomen as you breathe out. Continue this exercise for several minutes, or until you feel completely relaxed.

3. Rub the palms of your hands quickly, until they feel hot and then place your palms over your eyes (Fig 18.8).

4. Visualise a rainbow of Light (red, orange, yellow, green, blue, indigo and violet) spiralling down from the furthest reaches of space, entering the crown of your head, passing through your body and stretching deep into the ground. Feel the rainbow of Light rotating inside of you.

5. Maintaining the rainbow visualisation, place your hands back in gassho (prayer position) in front of your chest and silently say to yourself, or out loud, seven times, with meaning and purpose, "My faith keeps me strong, my courage helps me grow, no matter the situation my Light takes me home." As you speak these words visualise the rainbow of Light becoming brighter.

6. Place your palms over your eyes and repeat step 5.

Fig 18.8

Fig 18.9

Fig 18.10

Fig 18.11

7. Place your palms, on either side at the top of your chest and repeat step 5 (Fig 18.9).

8. Place your palms on either side of your lower chest (Fig 18.10) and repeat step 5.

9. Place your palms on either side covering you abdomen, middle fingers meeting the navel (Fig 18.11) and repeat step 5.

10. Place your palms at either side just below the navel (Fig 18.12) and repeat step 5.

Fig 18.12

11. Place your hands in the gassho (prayer position) in front of your chest and visualise the rainbow of Light passing through your body, turning into a wall of solid white Light, so you are absorbed in the Light.

12. Silently say to yourself, with meaning and purpose, three times, "My faith is infinite, the Light my guide that Light's my path, that Light's my way, I am truly grateful for each new day."

13. When you have finished, take a deep breath, in and out through your nose and then bow to the Universe.

Part Six

Being The Way

Chapter Nineteen

A Guide to Others

"If we submit to our true purpose we are all called upon in some way to work for the higher good, to take the hands of others and guide those hands to the Light. Fulfil your calling, be the way."

Reaching this point is a landmark in your journey and shows just how far you have come. Not everyone can be a beacon, to Light the way for others. Even those blessed with this very purpose, can often end up in a quandary when things do not turn out as they had expected. We can only do as much as we are granted by God or the Universe, but as a collection of sentient beings forming part of an overall 'oneness,' we owe it to each other and to our souls, to bring aid to those who are destined to fall upon our higher paths for help. So, if called to Light the path of others, fulfil your duty with delight.

Up until this point you will, most likely, have focused predominantly on developing yourself, but now is the time to show others what you have learned. You will not be showing everyone, but those individuals who are in the right place to hear the words, to know the truth and to follow their own higher paths in life. No preaching, just honesty, candidness, let others see that you are the epitome of truth and learn as you have learned. Let your strength helps others to gain strength. Let your courage be a bolster to those sent to you, who lack courage and empower them. Help other people see that they hold the key to their happiness and all that is required is that they take responsibility for themselves, love unconditionally and seek the truth in earnest. Be messengers of some of the truths of the Universe to those who are at the right place to listen and truly comprehend, to take forward and implement and to turn right words into right actions.

It is not always easy to help others, the rewards are far greater than anything money can buy, but you have to be totally prepared to share your knowledge wisely. Remember the earlier chapter on wisdom, everyone's path is different and everyone is on a different place on their path. Qualify your words according to the circumstances. There should not be any arrogance or berating, just humility and openness. This doesn't mean you should suffer fools gladly, just be who you really are, wherever you are. Be detached from people in a healthy way, care without caring, without being drawn into every single person's life, without taking on the pain of others.

Let your faith always guide you. It is all well and good re-inventing your life, but it can be difficult to know what to say, how to say it, when to say it and then you may wonder "but what will they think? Will they think I am insane?" It does not matter how other people perceive you, as long as you are connected to your intuition and fulfilling your purpose, it is no business of anyone else what you are doing. People are in no way permitted to judge, although they often do on a daily basis, without a second thought for their behaviour. If you have something you desperately need to say to someone and your intuition has told you to do so then do it without any hesitation. Let the words torrent from your mouth.

Sometimes, we have to tell people things they do not want to hear and we wonder if we are doing the right thing by telling them. On some occasions people have to face harsh truths whether they like it or not. Let me give you an example. Without making indiscriminate statements about all tarot card readers, there are some people practising this intuitive art that will simply tell people whatever they want to hear. They may either do this through politeness to avoid causing offence, or they may do it for monetary reasons. Of course, there are some things you should never tell an individual, for instance if you intuitively know that someone is going to lose their job, it would not be in their interests to inform them. You could though, encourage them to make positive changes in their life and perhaps learn some new skills.

Sometimes the best way to work can be to tell people the answer they need to hear, rather than the one they have chosen to ask. Someone may ask if they will get a new partner within the next year and what they may actually need to know is that they need to take steps in life to pursue their spiritual path.

Spiritual guidance is about showing people a door and then it's up to them whether they choose to walk through it or not. People often look for gurus who will tell them precisely what to do in every area of their life, but spiritual guidance is about encouraging people to trust in their own inner wisdom, rather than relying on someone else's.

Wisdom should be ever present when telling anyone anything and the consequences of those spoken words need careful consideration. We don't have a license to tell people anything we want to, paying no head to the repercussions, but one with deeply connected intuition, who has worked on their spiritual growth and reached the appropriate place spiritually, should have enough insight to pass on the **relevant wisdom** to the **right people**.

It is also vital not to answer any closed questions. If someone asks you, "will I leave my husband," don't give that person a direct answer. As I have previously discussed, none of us are gurus, we are here to hold out a hand but not to make people's choices for them, or tell them exactly what they will or won't do. If you possess wisdom, if you have found faith, then use it in the right way.

There are many occasions when we have to stand back from situations, rather than throwing ourselves into the thick of it. As enlightened beings, we should always avoid getting emotionally involved in other people's lives. We need to be detached, to see things from a much higher vantage point, to step outside the proverbial box and be objective. If you find yourself becoming emotionally entangled in a circumstance, then for goodness sake don't give any advice, because you will be in danger of mistaking your emotions for intuition and when this happens, everything can go horribly wrong.

It can be especially difficult with family, spouses and friends to be emotionally detached, because these are people close to you that you have a very strong bond with. As you learn to love everyone unconditionally and develop a higher state of awareness, you will be more readily able to detach from loved ones. Sometimes, telling a parent or friend some stark home truths is required and this is a real challenge, but a worthwhile one. If you can say your piece, this will not only further foster your spiritual growth and self-development, but help them too, in the long term. Always try to remain above it all, not in an aloof, arrogant way but in a higher, more divine way.

I cannot emphasise enough the necessity of remaining humble before God or the Universe, in working towards the goal of enlightenment. None of what I have said should be used as a manipulation tool, or as an ego booster to make others feel small and insignificant. We are all special and we all have a distinct purpose. We are all part of God, or the Universe or 'oneness,' however you would choose to term it and each of us has as much right to be here as anyone else, regardless of what our purpose is. Only once we become wise, can we impart real insight to anyone, otherwise we would be using our other faculties such as: emotions or human thought. By all means be confident and inspirational, but never let this turn to ego. You may exclaim "this would never happen to me!" but it does happen to some people.

There are some who have stepped on their spiritual path with very good intentions, but they have later allowed their ego to dupe their intuition and have ending up pursuing physical or emotional goals, rather than searching for their true spiritual nature. There is no need to obsess about every single thing, just implicitly trust your intuition and remain connected, so that you will always retain your humility and accept that we are all undergoing a learning process here. Regardless of how enlightened someone may be, they are still learning every single day of their life. **No human being is completely perfect**.

Helping others is something we should all be doing on a daily basis, whether it is by standing back from a situation, offering a listening ear, showing compassion, offering an objective viewpoint and so on. If we can foster meaningful kindness towards each other, towards every living thing, then we can develop ourselves, nourish our souls and contribute towards the positive development of society.

The twenty-first century seems to be a century of lots of lost, lonely, isolated, and largely selfish individuals. We need to be more benevolent towards each other, rather than just walking on by all the time and pretending that nothing is happening. The daydream needs to end, the pretence, the naivety. We need to make footprints in the sand, rather than burying our heads in it and just hoping that society's problems will disappear.

Society needs to wake up, quickly, before it is too late. Knowing you have made a difference, no matter how small, will enliven you and the imprints in the sand, that you have made, will nurture your soul. The Light that shines within you will glow so bright that all who come to know you, in some way, whether they realise it or not, will benefit from your deep connection, your insight, perception, your intuition. Be happy to be the way and know that you are becoming ever closer to achieving enlightenment.

There are four techniques below to strengthen your spirituality and to help you to help others. These exercises are entitled: Strength and Guidance in Helping Others, Standing Back, Retaining Humility in Your Spiritual Work and Being the Way.

The first exercise will help you to gain inner resolve that will radiate through to the people who cross your path. You will exude confidence, strength and wisdom and this will help you to empower other people, the way you have been empowered yourself.

This technique focuses on implanting courage to guide others into your head, heart and stomach or your physical, emotional and spiritual bodies.

The affirmation and prayer used will centre you and help you to be more forcefully guided in all your interactions with others. The prayer will further reinforce your connection with your true spiritual self, so that you formulate the right words to say and know whom to speak those words to. It will also help you to accept the 'oneness' that exists, the incredible link that joins us all together. Practise this exercise at least three or four times a week.

The second exercise, called Standing Back, will give you the foresight to be detached from situations and always maintain an objective viewpoint, or in essence a higher more divine perspective. By continual practise of this exercise, you will no longer become emotionally entangled in situations. You will develop far greater clarity and knowledge of when to say something, if you should say something and exactly what you should be saying.

The breathing exercise will help you to consciously, as well as subconsciously, relax and get your mind used to the suggestion of instant calm. If you practise this enough you should only have to think of the word 'calm' and you will immediately be placed into a more relaxed and intuitive state of mind. It really does work.

The box visualisation will assist you in developing a healthy detachment from those around you. This should allow you to maintain objectivity, something that many people find more difficult than they might be willing to admit. It really is so very important to be detached. Don't think that you are being selfish or uncaring. It has absolutely nothing to do with this. You are being much more caring by adopting a higher perspective and taking account of the bigger picture. Help with detachment and unconditional love and you will shoot along your higher, divine path with far greater ease and peace of mind. Staying detached is hard, but as you become more enlightened it will become much easier.

The third exercise, called Retaining Humility is about staying humble all the way through your journey. Be careful not to mistake confidence for arrogance. If ego creeps into your spiritual work, you will soon slip off your path into a completely different direction. This exercise will give you some quiet time by yourself, to reflect and give thanks for where you are in life now and where you will be in the future. It will enable you to help others without being dominating and overly wilful with people. Remember, stay detached but not in an arrogant way. The breathing exercise will not only assist you in attaining serenity, but it will additionally give you clearer vision and free your mind from clutter and any unnecessary burdening ego.

The affirmations will help you to always be your higher self in your daily life, to listen to your intuition, to know yourself, that you may know and help others to know, what is really important in life. Your body, mind and soul need to be heading in the same direction and all the exercises in this book, including this one, will foster your ability to be intuitive in every part of your life. Never be afraid of your intuition, it is your greatest gift. Practise this exercise as often as possible.

The final exercise focuses on consolidating what you have achieved from the previous exercises. It will give you the strength and courage you need to fulfil your higher path, stand your ground and show others their path, if they choose to be shown. As crazy as it may sound, not everyone wants to fulfil their highest potential, either because they are afraid of what this entails or because they see life as being easier if they don't take that leap of faith or the necessary risks.

You cannot and must not make anyone do anything they do not want to do. We are given the ability to make choices. This is what separates us from animals. As humans with the ability to make choices, we have responsibilities and at the end of the day it is up to us and us only, to do what we know we have to do. You can guide people but you cannot live another person's life for them. This exercise will help you to guide for the highest outcome, you can only do your best and then what will be, will be.

The breathing exercise will prove of great benefit to your lung capacity, as well as offering healing and relaxation. The patting used in this technique forms part of the healing process. By allowing yourself to be raised up into the Light, you will come to a point where you feel completely at peace and when saying the prayer used, you will mean it from the very central core of your being. This sincerity and earnest attitude will ensure that you work to the best of your ability. You will eventually, always be lead by your higher self and realise how blessed you are.

This exercise should be practised as often as possible. The more effort you put into your spiritual work, the more effort you will want to put into it. If you neglect your path, you will start to feel lost again and lacking in energy. See any obstacles as opportunities and allow the Universe to be your guide. As you practise these exercises on a regular basis, you will develop far greater clarity and focus and this will help you in every area of you life. We all need time to stop and be still. Grant yourself that time, you deserve it.

Exercises

Strength and Guidance in Helping Others

1. Lie in a comfortable position either on a yoga mat, on the floor or on your bed. Place your hands palms facing down on either side of your abdomen, so that your two middle fingers meet at your navel (Fig 19.1).

2. Breathe in and out very slowly and deeply through your nose, focusing on your abdomen gently rising as you breathe in and falling as you breathe out. Visualise pure white Light filling your head and remain focused on your stomach and head for several minutes or until you feel relaxed.

3. Place your right hand over your navel and your left hand at the top of your chest in the centre (Fig 19.2). Visualise the Light in your head travelling down into your lungs and chest area and into your stomach, then into your shoulders, arms and hands so eventually your entire body from head to your pelvic region is engulfed in Light.

4. Silently say to yourself, or out loud, with meaning and purpose, seven times, "May strength and guidance Light my way so that I may guide and help others be the same."

5. Place your palms directly over your eyes (Fig 19.3) and repeat the affirmation from step 4.

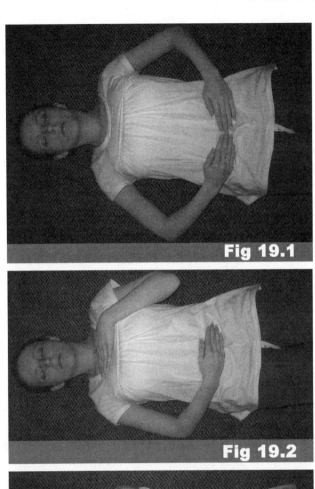

Fig 19.1

Fig 19.2

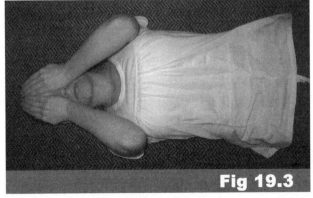

Fig 19.3

6. Place your hands in the gassho (prayer position) in front of your chest and either silently or out loud, recite the following prayer five times:

    May strength and honesty be my guide
    In life always never to hide
    My soul soaked in unconditional love
    Extended from me and the Life given above
    My hope is that I become my true spiritual self
    To be all I can to walk always with the wealth
    Of knowing that no money can buy
    The joy I have of my soul soaring high
    May I hold out my hand to the aid of others
    For in truth all humanity are of the One who loves us
    Let me be truth and show truth to all who must see
    God, the Light, the Universe to guide me to be.

7. Move yourself into a seated position, either on the floor in seiza (on your knees with your bottom resting on your heels) or in agura (cross-legged) or on a chair. Place your hands in gassho (prayer position) in front of your chest.

8. Take a slow, deep breath in and out, through your nose and allow Light to fill the entire room and your entire body. Spend a couple of minutes peacefully absorbed in the Light.

9. Bow to the Universe to finish.

Standing Back

1. Sit down comfortably either on the floor in seiza (on your knees with your bottom resting on your heels) or in agura (cross-legged) or on a chair. Make sure your back is straight. Place your hands in gassho (prayer position) in front of your chest.

2. Breathe in and out slowly and deeply, through your nose. On the in breath silently say to yourself, "breathe in calm" and on the out breath silently say to yourself, "breathe out stress." Continue with this process for three to fifteen minutes. Ensure that your shoulders and abdomen remain relaxed throughout this exercise and direct your focus to your tanden (about 3cm below the navel.)

3. Visualise yourself sitting inside a big brown box, which is empty, apart from you seated in the centre. See the hustle and bustle of people's daily lives going on around you, but feel separate and detached from it, almost as if you were a ghost and everything is going on around you, but no one can see or hear you.

4. Imagine yourself, your physical and spiritual bodies, growing in height and see yourself stretching out of the box, as you get taller and taller. The bustle of voices around you becomes quieter, as you reach through the sky. Peer at the people down below you and travel through the skies taking in the views of clouds, the wash of blue and birds flying by. See how distant everyone below you looks. Their voices are now inaudible. As your head enters space take in all the stars and planets, as you look down, the people below are so very tiny, just

197

minute dots in the box below. Keep moving upwards until you see a blinding Light and head for the Light taking in the full extent of its beauty.

5. Surrounded by Light with your feet back in the box, silently say to yourself, or out loud, with meaning and purpose, five times, "I stand above, detached from all situations. With a higher view granted by the Light, I can see clearly without attachment."

6. Allow your spiritual body to stay in the Light as pure white Light, whilst your physical body returns down to earth, back inside the box. Visualise yourself knocking down the walls of the box so no one inside, including you, is so trapped. Hear the voices of those around you become more distinctive, as if you could almost hear exactly what every single person was saying. Feel uplifted that you can help some of them and yet remain detached with your spirit in the Light.

7. Repeat five times the affirmation from step 5.

8. When you have finished, take a deep breath in and out through your nose, then bow to the Universe.

Retaining Humility

1. Sit down comfortably either on the floor in seiza (on your knees with your bottom resting on your heels) or in agura (cross-legged) or on a chair. Make sure your back is straight. Place your hands in gassho (prayer position) in front of your chest.

2. Breathe in and out deeply through your nose, closing your eyes as you breathe in for a slow count of seven and opening your eyes and staring straight ahead of you, as you breathe out for a slow count of seven. Continue this process seven times.

3. Place your palms over your eyes and continue the breathing pattern from step 2, seven times.

4. Place your hands back in gassho (prayer position) in front of your chest and silently say to yourself, or out loud, with meaning and purpose, seven times, "May the Light that guides me allow me to see, to Light the way of others and retain humility. May I be that Light."

5. Place your hands palms facing down on the crown of your head (Fig 19.4) and repeat the affirmation from step 4, seven times.

6. Place your left hand palm facing down over the centre of your chest and your right hand palm facing down over your navel (Fig 19.5) and repeat the affirmation from step 4, seven times.

7. Return your hands to gassho and repeat the affirmation from step 4, whilst slowly and gently opening and closing your eyes, throughout the affirmation.

8. When you have finished take a deep breath in and out, through your nose, then bow to the Universe.

Fig 19.4

Fig 19.5

Being The way

1. Lie in a comfortable position either on a yoga mat, on the floor or on your bed. Place your hands loosely at your sides and concentrate your mind on your tanden (3cm below your navel).

2. Breathe in very slowly through your nose, taking in as much air as you possibly can, so your stomach and lungs are completely filled with air. Breathe out through your mouth, as much as you possibly can until you feel you have completely emptied your stomach and lungs of air. After each out breath, gently pat your forehead three times with your left hand. Continue this pattern for a few minutes or until you feel completely relaxed.

3. Visualise your whole body levitating off the floor and floating up to the middle of the room. As you get to the middle, visualise white Light surrounding your entire body and gravitating from you outwards to fill up the whole room with Light.

4. Visualise the Light stretch above you towards the ceiling. As it does so, see the Light drawing you up higher with it. Allow yourself to be carried into the sky and then into space, all the while enshrined in and following the journey of the Light.

5. See yourself rise upwards as far as the eye can see. When you feel you have reached the pinnacle of the Light spend a few minutes relaxing, bathed in the warm glow that is enveloping your body.

6. Silently say to yourself, or out loud, with meaning and purpose, five times the following prayer:

   May I be an example, may my words be true
   That others may see the Light, as I have seen you
   May my words be all that my higher self wishes to bear
   That others who dare listen will be taken to theirs
   I am blessed in my path and I seek to fulfil my purpose
   Always and forever.

7. Gently sit up and place your hands in gassho (prayer position) in front of your chest and silently say to yourself, or out loud, five times, "May I live in the Light that the Light may lead me."

8. When you have finished, take a deep breath in and out, through your nose and then bow to the Universe.

Part Seven

Enlightenment

Chapter Twenty

At One

"When you travel down the tunnel you will see a symphony of colours and a Light so bright that you can barely dare to open your eyes, but you will, and then you will understand that enlightenment is yours and forever your soul will remain in peace."

Enlightenment, when our physical, emotional and spiritual bodies re-unite to form a perfect circle, a 'oneness' that has no beginning, middle or end but just sweet, complete perfection. What is it like to be here? No one can know unless they are enlightened, no one can truly comprehend until they reach this stage in their spiritual development. When they do finally arrive, they will comprehend that they have all the answers they could ever possibly need. There is no more discord, or inner battles between intuition and the rational mind; no more looking in the wrong places, because there is only harmony and deep, profound understanding of everything. There is a

Passage to Freedom

deep humility that knows no bounds, an awe-inspiring feeling of being part of something much greater than you are. There is absolutely nothing like it and everything else pales gingerly in comparison. To be enlightened is to be truly free and to break away from those chains that once tied you to this earth.

If you are indeed enlightened, there will be no need to question whether you are or not. The question will not even arise, certainty will prevail, humility will permeate your every move and honesty will be your guide. The enlightened, walk the earth but they are not really here, their souls walk free in heaven and they live each day to serve their higher purpose. Enlightenment is not something that is in the grasp of many, but it is achievable with deep dedication, a devoted spirit and a willingness to tread the correct path, whatever that might entail.

Being enlightened means having no obstacles to your inner guidance, no barriers to the ultimate freedom of your spirit, possessing profound insight and wisdom and knowing exactly how to use it, following your true purpose in earnest. Enlightenment is all these things and so much more. It is within our grasp, but so few reach out to grab it and so they suffer, sanctioned by their own soul, due to lack of any deep spiritual connection.

When we are enlightened, our intuition governs our every move and we always move willingly and with only our higher purpose in mind. Everything else in life is extraneous and fleeting and the enlightened are constantly aware of this. Trust, love, compassion, humility and deep unquestionable understanding takes precedence over human physicality. The feeling of pure love is completely overwhelming and it seeps into and out of our every pore.

There may be many who proclaim to understand these dizzy heights or even to have reached them, but in reality, so few have. Enlightenment brings peace, joy, unconditional love

206

and awareness, banishment of ignorance and an unyielding Light that burns within you. No one can put out this Light because those who try come from a place of ignorance, and in true enlightenment you come only from a place of love, truth and knowledge of the Universe. Peace, faith, humility and insight prevail, there is no more fear, no need to ask questions because all the answers are there and come to you readily, when you need them.

The enlightened have arisen from their human dream and they have witnessed the truth. Their blinkered vision is replaced with heightened senses and divine sight. Whilst the rest continue to walk in a drunken reverie, the enlightened doggedly attempt to wake them up, one by one, and work diligently on their life's purpose. They never give up because it is their destiny to persist, but they know that for all their efforts so many people will never even know they were asleep, or understand how to rise from their lifelong daydream.

To those individuals for whom enlightenment is but a heartbeat away, have infinite faith in yourself. You possess real wisdom. Don't let anyone try to turn you away from what you know to be true. With true enlightenment, you will not find answers from another human being but from God, or the Universe, or from your own intuition. Trust in and follow your higher path, dare to walk where the many fear to tread and the Light, unconditional love and the beauty of 'oneness' can be yours forever.

Be brave, challenge the views of others and always be yourself, wherever you find yourself. Blink and this life will be gone and you may have learned everything or nothing at all. Ultimately the choice is yours to make, but make the right one for you, not because anyone has told you to, but because you intuitively felt it was the right thing to do.

If you are reading this with a head full of questions and a bewildered expression, then work through the exercises in the other chapters over and over again until everything does make sense. Walk the path of the few who rise to the occasion, who see the truth above all else and who make the choices that will save them.

Do not scold yourself if you feel you are moving too slowly, or if you do not have all the answers you would like right away. Persistence and hard work will always pay off. You probably know a lot more than you think you do, just trust your intuition. Remember, your intuition is never wrong. By picking up this book and endeavouring to improve your life you have indicated a willingness and desire to be the best that you can be, so keep going and even when it seems tough, push on with greater enthusiasm. Your dedication will bring enlightenment when the time is right for you.

I have, in my past, pondered endlessly on many things and have even spent hours languishing over questions that I already had the answer to, only I hadn't looked deep inside myself. It can be all too easy to miss the signs that are shown to us. As human beings, we do not like change and we sit in a state of pointless self-denial, scared to look in-between the cracks. If you have come this far on your spiritual journey, if enlightenment is knocking at your door, then you have truly seen. I know that if you are here, you can see the signs. They don't just drift on by as you blindly follow the wrong trail. They appear to you in a blaze of glory.

We are always looking for something. We look for God and ask "where is God?" when God is within and all around us. We seek wisdom and chase others for the secrets to our deepest existence, but all we ever needed to do was to look right under our noses, to look in the mirror. When you can stop looking and you can see, hear, listen, then you can be enlightened. Then, the sun is brighter, the birds sing louder, the trees grow faster, the sky becomes bluer, beauty is more exquisite and a smile is more meaningful. If you chase nothing else in this life chase enlightenment and be sure to catch it and hold it dearly and eternally in the palm of your hand.

Does the soul need to transcend the physical body before enlightenment can be achieved? Well you do not need to die to reach nirvana, but your soul or higher self needs to be furnishing you with the purest guidance and your physical and emotional bodies need to be dominated by your higher self completely.

We should never make the assumption that someone has attained enlightenment because of their status or vocation, or because they proclaim great wisdom. Whether they are psychics, clairvoyants, mediums, intuitive counsellors, Reiki teachers or healers is irrelevant, if they do not live and think in the right way for their higher purpose on earth. A little bit of information or an ability to delve into the spiritual realm, has absolutely nothing to do with enlightenment. Look deeper and see people as they really are, rather than being fooled by the image they portray. Remember, that those who seek to manipulate others will find whatever arena is most conducive to being able to achieve this goal, and claiming to be a spiritual guru can have scope for abuse of position. Trust yourself, you have the answers.

There is no reason to assume that death precedes enlightenment or that enlightenment follows death. The souls of the deceased do not necessarily become wise and the living do not necessarily learn all their lessons. Our souls are on a journey. The time we spend here on earth forms a part of that journey and what we do while we are here is of the utmost importance. We choose to pass or fail an exam we set for ourselves along time ago. Enlightenment beckons, but at the same time ignorance can appear a safe adversary. What will you choose to do? Whatever choice you make, be prepared to accept that choice and the consequences. Enlightenment is the most exquisite state we can find ourselves in, if we are brave enough to embrace it.

You may or may not wonder if I consider myself to be spiritually enlightened. I feel that I am enlightened enough for where I need to be right now, but I never stop learning. I am not so bold as to proclaim that I have attained enlightenment, but I am getting there and one day I will reach my destination. Each day I express gratitude for where I am and sometimes I berate myself for not being more grateful. I am not perfect. I do not claim to be, but I strive towards perfection, to be more like God, to embody the unconditional love that I am.

I try to embrace the journey I am on. Sometimes it goes swimmingly, at other times it is fairly challenging, but I am completely on board with my higher path and every step I take, no matter how difficult, is worth the effort. I feel truly blessed and the more I know, the more I want to know, the more I cherish this journey I am on. It is breathtaking and it is a journey you can take yourself.

The three exercises below will aid you on your higher path to enlightenment and assist you in maintaining a high level of Universal understanding and awareness.

The first exercise called Enlightenment Transition, will aid you in seeing yourself as you really are; a very beautiful and enlightened soul. You will commit yourself to accepting and comprehending enlightenment and all that this entails.

The breathing exercise should help to deeply relax you and immerse you in Light, to increase your level of awareness and insight. Your physical, emotional and spiritual bodies will all become completely guided in time by your higher self and you will trust in your intuition completely.

The mirror image allows you to perceive yourself as you really are and to really know your own soul. By merging with the image, you can begin to realise your true potential. By repeating the first affirmation, you are starting to embrace enlightenment without fear. The second affirmation ensures that humility always prevails in the face of the higher power that guides, protects and unconditionally loves you.

The second exercise, Universal Knowledge will help you to understand that you have all the answers you could possibly need. Again, this will ensure that you always rely on your intuition and understand that the answers you seek are already within your grasp.

The Light flowing into your eyes will give you real wisdom and insight, helping you to shirk blinkered vision in favour of seeing the truth and recognising the consequences. Universal knowledge will forever be your greatest guide, if you practise this regularly enough.

The different hand positions used are to ensure that the affirmations and healing energy are implanted firmly into your body, mind and soul, so that you wholeheartedly believe in yourself. When Universal Knowledge is yours, never let anyone make you doubt yourself or make you question what you know to be true. Only doubt whatever does not sit right with your intuition.

The final exercise, Basking in the Light is a method for you to enjoy the glow of the energy and to be completely free and full of happiness. In essence, it permits you to escape from the harsh reality of the outside world and spend some time recuperating any lost energy, and recharging your batteries. Negative people and environments can cause a very adverse reaction in those who are enlightened. Imagine placing a Tibetan Monk, who has lived in mountain fresh air all his life, in the centre of a busy street in London and you get some idea of what it is like for an enlightened person to have to walk this earth. Toxins are in abundance so this wonderful exercise will help you to clear those toxins and re-focus.

Try to practise these exercises as often as you can. The third one should ideally be practised every day.

Exercises

Enlightenment Transition

1. Sit down comfortably
    either on the floor in
    seiza (on your knees
    with your bottom
    resting on your heels) or
    in agura (cross-legged)
    or on a chair. Make sure
    your back is straight.
    Place your hands in
    gassho (prayer position)
    in front of your chest.

Fig 20.1

2. Breathe in and out very
    slowly and deeply
    through your nose,
    whilst keeping your
    tongue touching the roof of your mouth. As you breathe
    in, visualise a beam of white Light coming down from as
    far above you as the eye can see, entering the top of your
    head, neck, shoulders and arms and working its way
    down your entire body. Remain like this for a few
    minutes or until you feel completely relaxed.

3. With your tongue still touching the roof of your mouth
    and maintaining the visualisation of the Light, place
    your right hand over your navel region and your left
    hand over your solar plexus region (Fig 20.1). Visualise
    the Light becoming brighter and brighter.

4. Visualise the Light expanding and filling the entire room, so you are bathed from every corner in a beautiful luminous glow. See yourself sitting opposite you within the Light, like a mirror image. The image of you is so bright that you can barely see it. See the image smiling at you and know that wisdom seeps from his / her every pore. Almost feel in awe of this image.

5. Visualise the beautiful image of you moving towards you and merging into your body. Feel one with the Light above and the beautiful spirit image that rests within you.

6. Silently say to yourself, or out loud, with meaning and purpose seven times, "The Light that shines within me knows that where my higher self leads enlightenment always follows. I embrace enlightenment with all that I am."

7. Place your hands back in gassho (prayer position) in front of your chest and repeat the affirmation from step 6, seven times.

8. Rest your hands palms facing upwards in your lap and again repeat the affirmation from step 6, seven times.

9. Silently say to yourself, or out loud, with meaning and purpose, "I am humble in the face of the greater power around me. I reach for humility, intuition and truth. May I be guided here always."

10. When you have finished, take a deep breath in and out through your nose, relax your tongue, and then bow to the Universe.

Universal knowledge

1. Lie in a comfortable position either on a yoga mat, on the floor or on your bed. Place your hands palm facing down on either side of your abdomen so that your two middle fingers meet at your navel (Fig 20.2).

2. Breathe in and out slowly and deeply through your nose, feeling your abdomen rise as you breathe in and fall as you breathe out. Also be aware of the passage of the air in and out of your body, focusing on the air entering your nostrils as you breathe in and tickling the very top of your lip as you breathe out. Continue with this process for a few minutes, or until you feel completely relaxed.

3. Place your hands over your eyes, palms covering the eyes (Fig 20.3) and visualise a bright beam of white Light coming down from as far above as the eye can, entering the top of your head, flowing down your neck and shoulders, along your arms and out of your hands into your eyes. Maintain this visualisation.

4. Silently say to yourself, or out loud, with meaning and purpose, nine times, "Please allow me to see all that I need to see and let Universal Knowledge forever guide me."

5. Place your hands at the sides of your head so your palms cover your temples (Fig 20.4) and repeat the affirmation from step 4, nine times.

6. Place your hands around your throat so your palms cup your throat (Fig 20.5) and repeat the affirmation from step 4, nine times.

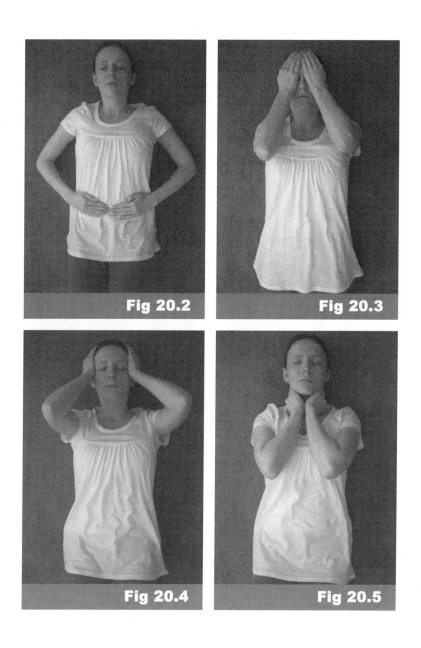

Fig 20.2

Fig 20.3

Fig 20.4

Fig 20.5

7. Place your hands at the back of your head, so your palms cup the base of your skull (Fig 20.6) and repeat the affirmation from step 4, nine times.

8. Place your hands either side at the top of your chest, palms facing down (Fig 20.7) and repeat the affirmation from step 4, nine times.

9. Place your hands either side underneath your chest so your little fingers touch the bottom of your ribcage (Fig 20.8) and repeat the affirmation from step 4, nine times.

Fig 20.6

10. Place your hands at either side of your navel, so your middle fingers meet at your navel (Fig 20.9) and repeat the affirmation from step 4, nine times.

11. Place your hands at either side just underneath your navel (Fig 20.10) and repeat the affirmation from step 4, nine times.

12. When you have finished, bring yourself up to a seated position, place your hands in gassho (prayer position) in front of your chest and gently bow to the Universe.

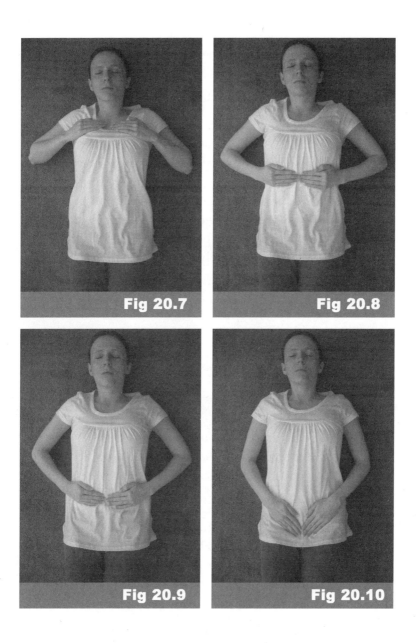

Fig 20.7

Fig 20.8

Fig 20.9

Fig 20.10

Basking in Light

1. Sit down comfortably either on the floor in seiza (on your knees with your bottom resting on your heels) or in agura (cross-legged) or on a chair. Make sure your back is straight. Have your hands palms facing upwards in your lap.

2. Breathe in slowly and deeply through your nose for a count of seven, visualising white Light entering your nostrils and filling your lungs. Breathe out for a count of seven, visualising the white Light permeating your entire body. Continue with this process for five to ten minutes, or until you feel completely relaxed.

3. Visualise that in your two relaxed palms, you have two glowing balls of white Light (Fig 20.11). Feel their shape, intensity and magnetism. Sit for a few minutes as you imagine these white balls of Light growing larger, until they are the size of two footballs.

4. Gently raise your arms up in front of you, as if lifting the globes of Light upwards (Fig 20.12). When you reach chest height, turn your palms to face inwards and bring them closer together, so that the two balls of Light merge into one giant beach ball sized globe of Light (Fig 20.13).

5. Raise your arms up over your head, carefully still visualising the ball of Light between your hands and gently place the ball of Light over your head (Fig 20.14). Allow your palms to relax back into your lap, palms facing upwards.

Fig 20.11

Fig 20.12

Fig 20.13

Fig 20.14

6. Imagine your head right in the middle of the globe of Light, which then expands in all directions. Visualise it expanding, little by little until eventually, you are surrounded by a giant globe of Light. Allow the globe to get bigger and bigger until it reaches far up towards space and deep down into the ground. Eventually, it should become so huge that you can no longer see where it begins and where it ends.

7. Silently say to yourself, or out loud, with meaning and purpose, three times, "Forever more I am bathed in Light, trusting always my intuition and possessing foresight. I am always open to the highest guidance and follow that guidance implicitly."

8. Place your hands in gassho (prayer position) in front of your chest. Remember exactly who you are and make a mental note to always remember this wherever you are.

9. Bow to the Universe to finish.

Part Eight

The Reiki Way

Chapter Twenty One

Reiki Lights The Way

"Reiki is not just another complementary therapy, Reiki is The Way of the Universe."

Nothing on this earth has changed my life more than Active Reiki. If it were not for this amazing healing system, I would probably be in a totally different place right now, physically, emotionally and spiritually. Out of everything I have ever achieved in my life, nothing has been more worthwhile than learning, practising and teaching this form of Reiki.

My Reiki comes above everything else, because it is the mainstay of my higher path. Had Reiki not beckoned me to pursue my true purpose, I have no doubt that I would be in a sorry place right now. Every time I teach Reiki to another student or give a Reiki treatment I become more amazed by its limitless potential. I personally do not believe that there is anything in this world that can induce such phenomenal life transformations. To put into words, the difference Reiki can make to a person is almost impossible. It is one of those things that you cannot quite understand until you experience it for yourself.

Why is Reiki so Special?

There are a number of ways to make enlightenment a reality, but realistically, as human beings, we have so many emotional blockages to our personal and spiritual growth. Many people are in blatant self-denial and often do not believe that they have any emotional blockages to begin with. Others know that they have much to work on, but despite concerted efforts they make little progress. Some people meditate for years on end, without coming anywhere near enlightenment.

Society generally speaking, has come so far away from its true spiritual origins that any frantic attempts to claw back what it has squandered often end up in vain. Humanity has largely disintegrated into a disconnected and confused bunch of individualistic people, who frequently replace spirituality with ego and vanity. Of course, I do not speak for everyone. There are people, who despite life's upheavals have remained true to their higher self and spiritual roots, but this is very rare and I posit that it becomes rarer with every second of every day.

You may proclaim me to be somewhat of a pessimist, but I like to consider myself as more of a realist. On a regular basis, people crush their abandoned souls, either unwittingly or apathetically. Reiki helps to provide the missing link to those who are searching for it. Reiki reconnects us to our true spiritual nature in a very short space of time. Then what we choose to do with that connection is entirely up to us.

You may well ask, "Well how is Reiki going to help with any of this?" I will do my very best to explain. In terms of the context of this book, Reiki, if taken as a course can be used along with the exercises I have given to enhance your personal and spiritual growth rapidly. Not everyone will learn Reiki and not everyone who does learn Reiki will use it frequently. As with anything, complete dedication is required to achieve spectacular results.

This is not a book about Reiki so I will not launch into laborious detail, but I will break down the fundamentals of how Reiki works and why Reiki has changed people's lives the world over.

I would like to stress that the Reiki used needs to be Active Reiki, to be effective, as was originally taught by the founder Mikao Usui. This will enable you to work directly on any physical, emotional and spiritual conditions.

Many Reiki practitioners use Reiki in a very passive way. This implies that they don't use Reiki to directly work on physical or emotional conditions, but instead act as channels, without putting any thought, focus or effort into the healing process. I have personally found Active Reiki to be far more effective. If in doubt, listen to your intuition when choosing a practitioner or teacher and ask plenty of questions. If they are unable to answer them appropriately, look elsewhere.

Reiki: A Reconnection Takes Place

Reiki is a natural form of energy healing, originating from Japan, in the early 1900s. Put very simply, naturally occurring, external, variable frequency energy is channelled through the healer's hands, into the client, to work on specific problems or conditions, whether they are physical, emotional or spiritual.

I believe that when we develop illnesses or injuries, we also manifest a corresponding frequency imbalance within our bodies or within our auras. Reiki works to bring the damaged body area or the emotion back to its ideal frequency. It might sound a little abstract or complicated but I can promise you, that in reality, it is incredibly easy. The main thing you need to know is that Reiki can help to heal on all levels.

Reiki consists of two words, 'Rei,' meaning spiritual or God's Highest Consciousness and 'Ki' meaning Life force energy that exists both within all living things and around all living things. According to the philosophy of Usui Reiki and many Eastern philosophies, if we are to be completely healthy 'Ki' needs to flow freely throughout our bodies. If our 'Ki' is unable to flow properly we can potentially develop an illness or injury.

The Japanese traditionally defined Reiki as 'spiritual energy' but it has come to have many differing interpretations. When we say Reiki nowadays, it refers to the traditional Usui System of Natural Healing. However, be aware that many people have tried to stamp their own mark on Reiki and there are now over a 144 different types of Reiki, some of which have nothing to do with the system of healing Mikao Usui taught, whatsoever.

The founder Mikao Usui discovered this system of healing whilst on a twenty-one day retreat of fasting, praying, meditating and chanting upon Mount Kurama in Japan. On the twenty-first day, he claims to have been given the Reiki cure and instant enlightenment along with the ability to heal using Universal energy. Prior to this, most healers had used their own internal life force energy or 'Ki' to heal with. This results in the healer's energy becoming terribly depleted and they can very often develop poor health. Other healers had worked purely on a spiritual level.

Reiki is completely unique in that it offers the ability to heal on all levels: physical, emotional and spiritual. Some people are natural healers and in these cases, they will either be using their own internal life force energy to heal with, or they will be channelling spiritual, higher frequency energy.

Active Reiki provides the ability to adapt the frequency of the energy to the condition(s) being treated.

Mikao Usui did not just haplessly stumble across this healing art; he had devoted his whole life to improving his body, mind and spirit. He was born into a Samurai family at a time when The Meiji Emperor had turned Japan from a feudal society to a democracy. The Samurai class had been stripped of their status.

Mikao Usui spent many years overcoming adversity. None the less, he was a very forward thinking gentleman and didn't let culture dictate his beliefs. In fact, he believed from an early age that all religions were really one religion. If you take out all the ritual and dogma and retain the core messages, there are a few fundamental beliefs. These basically amount to **right living** and **right thinking**.

Mikao Usui developed five precepts for his students to live their lives by and in their Western form these are:

Just for today, I will let go of anger
Just for today, I will let go of worry
Just for today, I will give thanks for my many blessings
Just for today, I will be kind to my neighbour and every living thing.

There is a deeper meaning within these precepts that Mikao Usui expected his students to discover for themselves, but ultimately they represented to him, the true meaning of religion without all the inflexibility and paraphernalia. Mikao Usui's students fondly referred to him as Usui Sensei, even before he discovered Reiki. A Sensei in Japan is a teacher or master who has great respect from his students.

Mikao Usui spent much of his time studying and was well versed in: Christianity, Buddhism, Shintoism, medicine, philosophy, psychology, mysticism and Kiko (a method of healing using your own internal energy).

After his discovery, spreading Reiki and the awareness of Reiki became Mikao Usui's primary concern. He had found instant enlightenment and wanted to share with others how they too could reach enlightenment, with the help of Reiki. Mikao Usui referred to Reiki as "the secret method of inviting happiness, the miraculous medicine of all diseases" and he wanted this healing therapy spread all over the world.

The Vital Connection

One of the most significant elements of a Reiki course is the attunement process. This is a method where a Reiki teacher connects the student to 'Universal Energy' or 'God's energy' to use for healing purposes. In the first chapter, I described how we all originally begin in a state of 'oneness,' but as life affects us and we make wayward choices, we become disconnected from our spiritual nature, from God. Our physical, emotional and spiritual bodies, instead of all heading in one direction, veer off on incredibly divergent paths and we are left feeling very confused and empty.

Establishing a re-connection to our true spiritual selves is not an easy thing to do, especially as we are so conditioned by society, our upbringing and our emotional traumas. Even those looking in the right areas can still end up totally lost.

The attunement process used in Reiki is a method to re-connect the student to God or the Universe, without years of meditation, praying or such like. Straight away, that person is connected to their intuition and has the ability to self-heal, heal others and head more rapidly towards enlightenment. Of course, whether or not that person does become enlightened depends on how much self-healing they do every day.

Some individuals prefer to take the whole process very slowly and make subtle changes in their life, bit by bit. Others, by nature of their higher path, move very quickly and make dramatic changes, self-heal regularly and become enlightened in a short space of time. How short? Well that depends on the person. It could be a day, a week, a month, or a year or more depending on who the person is and what their higher path on this earth entails.

This attunement process is how students are able to access Universal energy for healing, as opposed to using their own 'Ki' or life force energy for healing. By doing this, Reiki students will never deplete their own life force energy when they give healing. In fact, as they channel the energy through themselves into the client they receive healing themselves in the process.

The Reiki attunements radically elevate the student's own vibrational frequency, bringing them closer to God or the source of the energy. The higher our frequency is, the more spiritual we are. This gives the students more awareness, a heightened ability to perceive the bigger picture and makes them stronger channels for the energy. The more self-healing a student does, the better they will be as a healer and the more enlightened they will become. They will very quickly become far more intuitive, gain much clearer focus and vision and feel more guided by the Universe and better able to make healthy choices for themselves. The guiding signs in life become like a giant billboard saying, "head this way" and the students can decide for themselves if they want to follow their higher paths.

I can explain away the attunements, but the only way to truly comprehend how they work is to experience them. Receiving an attunement is like having years of burden lifted off your shoulders. It makes you feel like you sat in darkness for your entire life and then someone came and switched the light on, showing you the most exquisite and beautiful thing in the world. You are suddenly overcome with joy because finally you can see it. You can sometimes achieve in an instant, what people spend their entire lives trying to achieve, without success.

I have barely scratched the surface with what Reiki is all about, but I just wanted to give you a taster and hopefully for some of you the incentive to go and try out, or learn Reiki for yourself. There are millions of Reiki healers worldwide and there are even some paid Reiki practitioners working in NHS hospitals in the UK. I believe, or at least hope that it is only a matter of time before Reiki receives more recognition by medical professionals. Reiki is a fast track to enlightenment, if you choose to use it on yourself regularly and make good choices for your higher path in life.

Reiki can wipe away years of accumulated emotional traumas and societal restraints. Reiki can also help to improve physical conditions. Reiki can do all this and so much more. Mikao Usui was bestowed with an amazing gift to share with the world, a gift that would change people's lives the world over and help those who took it into their hearts to climb out of the quagmire and head up to heaven, where they belong. Life doesn't suddenly become perfect after learning Reiki, but it becomes far more beautiful and you can come to learn what it means to truly be happy and to truly be free.

The End Is The Beginning

Conclusion

Sometimes, it can be extremely difficult to see any good in the world. There are shocking atrocities happening every single day, there are vast numbers of individuals walking the streets with no sense of conscience or morality. They will readily tell a destructive lie, as if it means nothing. Society is governed by people who crave power for power's sake, people who hunger for their ever-expanding egos to be caressed and buffered by those around them.

If you look carefully enough you can see and smell the corruption, sleaze, grime and the blazing fire lit by humanity that devours everything in its path. History has failed to teach most humans anything new, for constantly the same mistakes are made over and over again. Evolution has not resulted in the evolving of souls. True unconditional love and compassion have proved to be qualities of the few, rather than features of the masses.

This is the grim reality of the world in which we live. Remember to perceive the truth and not simply what you would wish to see. Remember to see people as they really are, rather than how you would like them to be. Face up to reality instead of shying away. There is pain and suffering and cruel unjustified torture. It won't disappear because we choose to ignore it.

Though it is tainted, there is still so much beauty in the world. The lush planet earth we were tasked with nurturing is spectacular. The sun illuminates the sky in the morning, the birds sing out a dazzling chorus, the trees whisper softly in the breeze and you can feel the splendour surrounding you, if you dare to stop, to look and to listen. We get so lost in our day to day living, in the survival of the fittest and the grind of the rat race that we forget what we are here for. We forget every day that we were tasked with nurturing this exquisite world. We forget accidentally, or we choose to forget. Remember that we choose, it is our God given right and we do it for better or for worse till death do us part.

For some people, who have taken a deep breath and tentatively opened their eyes and ears, their calling beckons loud and clear. Unconditional love is as instinctive to them as taking a breath, as taking a step. Their compassion Lights up where there is usually darkness. In earnest, they try to recover what has been lost and make a desperate attempt to do what they can, for whom they can. In all the bleakness they do this still because they know that there is something worth saving in this world. The cesspool is enshrouded below a sky formed from a symphony of colours and a pure unrivalled love that knows no bounds and loves, regardless of circumstances.

There are souls that have great potential and though their inner Light is but a flicker of a flame, those who truly see, know that the flame can get brighter and it can be restored to a roaring fire of beautiful white Light. For those who dare to release their true potential there is a great deal of Light to be had amongst the darkness. There is much work to be done, so little time to do it and so few who even dare to stop and think about it, let alone actually go ahead and strive for it.

The key is to be able to see both the inimitable glorious joys of this earth and the soul destroying, crippling, decadence and destruction. Open your eyes so wide that you can't even blink and miss a second of what is going on in the world, so wide that they sting with incredulity at what rests before you, both in love and compassion and pain and torment.

Allow your ears to be sensitive to the subtlest sounds and never oblivious to what is going on around you. Speak what you know to be the truth and do so gladly with humility and passion. Dedicate yourself to improving your body, mind and spirit. Let this be your daily escapade, live and enjoy it. Do what you know to be right. Make healthy choices that nourish you and fuel your spiritual growth and development. Be hopeful but realistic. Be overjoyed but understated. Be all that you can be and don't be afraid of others' perceptions of the real you. Love yourself and love every single living thing, unconditionally. Walk the line of the words you speak, don't preach and fall into the betrayal of your higher self and those around you. Know that enlightenment will set you free. Truly observe, dare to open up to your intuition and set your soul free, so that your soul may fly and so that you may walk the passage to freedom.

The journey is just beginning and it is beautiful.

About The Author

Dawn Mellowship is a Reiki practitioner and teacher. As well as treating a wide range of clients, she has taught Reiki to hundreds of students, helping them to transform their lives and use Reiki for the benefit of themselves and others. Dawn devotes her life to her own personal spiritual growth and promoting health and well-being to as many people as she can. Her Reiki work has been featured in a host of publications including: Health and Fitness, Positive Health, Natural Health and Beauty and TNT. Dawn is also a journalist and as Features Editor of a health and lifestyle magazine called Tonic, she regularly contributed articles about poignant issues and living a healthy, happy lifestyle.

B O O K S

O books
O is a symbol of the world, of oneness and unity. In
different cultures it also means the "eye", symbolizing
knowledge and insight, and in Old English it means "place
of love or home". O books explores the many paths of
understanding which different traditions have developed
down the ages, particularly those today that express
respect for the planet and all of life.

Colours of the Soul
Transform your life through colour therapy
June McLeod
A great book, the best I've read on the subject and so inspirational.
Laura, Helios Centre
One of those books that makes a deep and lasting impression on our lives. **Chrissy Wright**
1905047258 176pp + 4pp colour insert **£11.99 $21.95**

Crystal Prescriptions
The A-Z guide to over 1,200 symptoms and their healing crystals
Judy Hall
2nd printing
Another potential best-seller. This handy little book is packed as tight as a pill-bottle with crystal remedies for ailments. It is written in an easy-to-understand style, so if you are not a virtuoso with your Vanadinite, it will guide you. If you love crystals and want to make the best use of them, invest in this book as a complete reference to their healing qualities.
Vision
1905047401 176pp 2 colour **£7.99 $15.95**

Grow Youthful
A practical guide to slowing your ageing
David Niven Miller
Over the millennia, many extraordinary people have lived well beyond a century. This easy to understand book reveals many of the secrets. Supported by recent scientific research, it cuts through much of the jargon and conflict concerning health and longevity.
1846940044 224pp **£10.00 $19.95**

The Healing Power of Celtic Plants
Healing herbs of the ancient Celts and their Druid medicine men
Angela Paine
Each plant is covered here in depth, explaining its history, myth and symbolism and also how to grow, preserve, prepare and use them. Uniquely, here, their properties are examined together with the scientific evidence that they work.
1905047622 304pp 250/153mm b/w illustrations **£16.99 $29.95**

The Healing Sourcebook
Learn to heal yourself and others
David Vennells
Here is the distilled wisdom of many years practice; a number of complementary therapies which are safe, easy to learn from a book, and combine wonderfully with each other to form a simple but powerful system of healing for body and mind.
1846940052 320pp **£14.99 $22.95**

Healing the Eternal Soul
Insights from past life and spiritual regression
Andy Tomlinson
Written with simple precision and sprinkled with ample case examples this will be an invaluable resource for those who assist others in achieving contact with the eternal part of themselves. It is an invaluable contribution and advancement to the field of Regression Therapy. More so, it is an incredibly interesting read! **Dr. Arthur E. Roffey**, Past Vice-President, Society for Spiritual Regression
190504741X 288pp **£14.99 $29.95**

Humming Your Way to Happiness
An introduction to Tuva and overtone singing from around the world
Peter Galgut
An engaging tour of the field by a medical scientist that takes the reader

into the cross-cultural landscape of sound, with special emphasis on Tuva and overtone singing. The author puts his journey into a wide context so that the reader can understand the role that sounds have played in various parts of the world, and also considers sounds, music and religions as well as the use of sound therapy. **Scientific and Medical Network Review**
1905047142 144pp **£9.99 $19.95**

The Invisible Disease
The dangers of environmental illnesses caused by electromagnetic fields and chemical emissions
Gunni Nordstrom
Highly recommended. This most informative and well written book makes the connections between the ranges of illnesses and chemicals used in the manufacture of modern appliances that are mistakenly considered safe. They are not. **Luminous Times**
1903816718 256pp **£9.99 $14.95**

Masters of Health
The original sources of today's alternative therapies
Robert van de Weyer
More and more people have been turning to alternative approaches to health and illness, especially those that have been tried and tested over many centuries. Here are the major original texts, from eastern and western traditions, rendered into modern idiom. With introductions to each, they form a summary of ancient wisdom on human wholeness.
1905047150 192pp **£9.99 $19.95**

The Theorem
A complete answer to human behaviour
Douglas Arone
Arguably the genius of any great discovery lies in its originality-a fresh idea that is set to challenge traditional modes of thinking while advancing

man's march along the path of progress. Far from the idea that the human foetus is cocooned from the cares and woes of existence, our first experience of fear, joy and sorrow actually precedes our birth. This in a nutshell is what this book is set to tell the world. (The author) has accomplished his task with exceptional brilliance. **B. K. Abolade MD; MRCP** (UK), Child and Adolescent Psychiatrist, Alabama
190504710X 496pp **£19.99 $39.95**

Universal Principles and the Metamorphic Technique
The keys to healing and enlightenment
Gaston St-Pierre
It has slowly and quietly gained respect from not only those whose lives have been transformed by it, but from doctors and specialists impressed with the results for conditions ranging from doctors and specialists impressed with the results for conditions ranging from dyslexia to eating disorders. **Lorna V.** *The Sunday Times*

Thousands who have experienced the technique affirm that life is never the same once you step onto the metamorphic path. **Jane Alexander**, *Daily Mail*
1903816602 308pp **£11.99 $19.95**

A-Z of Reiki Pocketbook
Everything About Reiki
Bronwen and Frans Stiene
A-Z of Reiki, the latest work by Bronwen and Frans Stiene, is an all-encompassing and expansive glossary of Reiki and Japanese healing. This book helps clear the way for everyone to partake of Reiki. **Nina Paul**, author of *Reiki for Dummies*
1905047894 272pp 125/90mm **£7.99 $16.95**

Energy Works!
Initiation without a master
Teresa Parrott and Graham Crook

Graham and Teresa have explored the world of SKHM to a depth that few have been able to achieve, and, most importantly, they have been able to share their experience with others through their words in the most beautiful way. Those who read about their experience will be initiated in a journey of the heart. I highly recommend allowing yourself to experience that journey. **Patrick Zeigler**
1905047525 304pp £12.99 $24.95

Healing Hands
Simple and practical reflexology techniques for developing god health and inner peace
David Vennells

Promising good health and inner peace, this practical guide to reflexology techniques may not be a glossy affair but it is thoroughly and clearly illustrated. Hand reflexology isn't as well known as the foot variety, but it's undeniably effective and, perhaps most usefully, it's a technique that can be applied for self-treatment. Whatever the healing process is that you're going through, whenever you're experiencing it, Healing Hands can support your journey. **Wave**
1905047126 192pp £9.99 $16.95

The Japanese Art of Reiki
A practical guide to self healing
Bronwen and Frans Stiene
2nd printing

This is a sequel to the aclaimed "Reiki Sourcebook." For those of us in the West who see adverts for weekend Reiki Master courses and wonder about the authenticity of the tradition, this book is an eye-opener. It takes the reader back to the Japanese roots of the tradition in a way that conveys its inspirational power and cultural flavour. The book is illustrated and is full of practical guidance for both practitioners and general

readers. **Scientific and Medical Network Review**
1905047029 208pp **£12.99 $19.95**

Reiki Jin Kei Do
The way of compassion and wisdom
Steve Gooch

Steve Gooch has done an excellent job in presenting to the public the world's first book on the deeply profound and beautiful teachings that were given to me by Seiji Takamori. In doing so he has become the spokesperson for the whole lineage. I recommend it highly to all.
Dr Ranga Premaratna, Lineage Head of Reiki Jin Kei Do
1905047851 240pp **£12.99 $21.95**

Reiki Mastery
For second degree students and masters
David Vennells
3rd printing
A compassionate, wise, handbook to making the most of the Life Force Energy that surrounds and informs us all.
An excellent reference for anyone interested in hands-on healing. Helpful and insightful, good and solid. **Amazon**
190381670X 192pp **£9.99 $14.95**

Reiki Q&A: 200 Questions & Answers for Beginners
Lawrence Ellyard
2nd printing
This unique handbook clearly answers all kinds of questions about Reiki and its practice as well as dispelling any misconceptions. Useful, dependable and highly recommended. **Penny Parkes**, author of *15-minute Reiki*
1905047479 208pp **£12.99 $24.95**

Reiki Techniques Card Deck
Heal Yourself Intuitively
Bronwen and Frans Stiene

Everyone has the ability to initiate self-healing-it is your birthright. The techniques in this deck of 45 cards, selected from the most effective traditional and non-traditional Reiki techniques from around the globe, offer you the opportunity to consciously tap into your healing ability, supporting you on your natural path.

1905047193 24pp + 40 colour cards, box 88/127mm **£15.99 $24.95**

Ultimate Reiki Guide for Practitioners and Masters
Lawrence Ellyard

2nd printing

In this excellent volume, Lawrence Ellyard brings together his considerable expertise and experience to provide a clear and concise view of how to conduct Reiki and to establish oneself as a Reiki practitioner. It will be invaluable for all Reiki professionals and lay persons as a spiritual, practice and business guide. **Dr. Ralph Locke**, CEO, Ikon

1905047487 208pp **£12.99 $24.95**

The Reiki Sourcebook
Bronwen and Frans Stiene

5th printing

It captures everything a Reiki practitioner will ever need to know about the ancient art. This book is hailed by most Reiki professionals as the best guide to Reiki. For an average reader, it's also highly enjoyable and a good way to
learn to understand Buddhism, therapy and healing. **Michelle Bakar**, *Beauty magazine*

1903816556 384pp £12.99 $19.95

Your Reiki Treatment
Bronwen and Frans Stiene

This is the first title to look at Reiki from the client's perspective. Whether you are searching for relaxation, healing, or spiritual growth, a Reiki treatment can be a revelation. Find out how to make the most of it. Learn how to prepare, what to expect, and how to continue furthering your personal growth after the treatment is finished.

18469490133 240pp **£9.99 $19.95**

Back to the Truth
5,000 years of Advaita

Dennis Waite

A wonderful book. Encyclopedic in nature, and destined to become a classic. **James Braha**

Absolutely brilliant...an ease of writing with a water-tight argument outlining the great universal truths. This book will become a modern classic. A milestone in the history of Advaita. **Paula Marvelly**

1905047614 500pp **£19.95 $29.95**

Don't Get MAD Get Wise
Why no one ever makes you angry, ever!

Mike George

There is a journey we all need to make, from anger, to peace, to forgiveness. Anger always destroys, peace always restores, and forgiveness always heals. This explains the journey, the steps you can take to make it happen for you.

1905047827 160pp **£7.99 $14.95**